Buying Creative Services

BOBBI BALDERMAN

Printed on recyclable paper

NTC Business Books
a division of *NTC Publishing Group* • Lincolnwood, Illinois USA

Library of Congress Cataloging-in-Publication Data

Balderman, Bobbi, 1946–
   Buying creative services / Bobbi Balderman.
      p. cm.
   Includes index.
   ISBN 0-8442-3497-4
   1. Advertising media planning—Cost effectiveness. 2. Advertising
layout and typography—Cost effectiveness. I. Title.
HF5825.B28   1995
659.1'029'7—dc20   95-11299
                                                          CIP

Published by NTC Business Books, a division of NTC Publishing Group
4255 West Touhy Avenue
Lincolnwood (Chicago), Illinois 60646-1975 U.S.A.
© 1996 by NTC Publishing Group. All rights reserved.
No part of this book may be reproduced, stored in a retrieval system,
or transmitted in any form or by any means,
electronic, mechanical, photocopying, recording or otherwise,
without the prior permission of NTC Publishing Group.
Manufactured in the United States of America.

5 6 7 8 9 BC 9 8 7 6 5 4 3 2 1

CONTENTS

PREFACE

If you are a small-business owner, marketing director, communications manager, human resources director, product manager, fund-raiser, or administrative assistant, or if you are in a position to purchase marketing or communications tools, *Buying Creative Services* was written for you. It was written in response to cries for help from a long list of friends, clients, and colleagues who, at some point, have felt helpless or overwhelmed when trying to buy creative services.

Buying Creative Services will take out the mystery, eliminate the headaches, and enhance feelings of success involved in an otherwise challenging task.

I have worked in the advertising business for more than twenty-six years. I began realizing that I was spending a great deal of time educating my clients about what exactly they were buying from me and my suppliers.

It became obvious that these people needed help. The horror stories I have heard about mistakes that have been made in buying creative services could fill the pages of this book. For example, people have chosen printers merely on price, only to find that the final bill doubled.

Perhaps you can relate to the experience of people who have received printing bids so diverse that it was impossible to determine which one was correct or appropriate. After speaking to these same people further, I regularly discovered that they had not given all their suppliers the same information. No wonder they were confused.

If you can identify with any of these people, this book is going to keep you from making the same mistakes. Your horror stories will become success stories.

Whether you need a small ad for a local publication, a brochure for a product your company has developed, a sales training video, or possibly a national advertising campaign, you will be faced with the same challenge—namely, how do you get it done? The solutions may seem more complex and confusing than meets the eye. Knowing the answer to the question, "How do I get this done?" not only can simplify the process, but also can ultimately save you grief and money.

As in any project, there are many pieces that make up the whole. In the case of buying creative services, sometimes the pieces are not as clearly defined, making the purchasing decisions more difficult.

It is not as simple as, for example, buying a car. When purchasing a car, you usually have an idea of your budget. You know what colors and features you like and what style appeals to you. You visit several dealers, negotiate a price, and drive away. Buying is not so easy when you aren't sure of the budget, you don't know exactly what you need or how many you should order, or you have no idea who should help you get the job done.

My favorite question that I am asked all the time is, "How much is a brochure, anyway?" I usually answer, "How much is a suit?" Seems ridiculous doesn't it? But it makes a point. There are many variables in buying any marketing or communications tool, just as there are in buying suits. Having some idea up front of what you want makes the shopping a lot easier.

Producing a communications or marketing tool does not have to be your biggest nightmare. Once you have clearly defined your objectives and goals, there are numerous creative service professionals trained to assist you. Or, with the proper computer and software and a little knowledge, there are certain things you can even do yourself.

Whatever the project, whether small or large, you need to get out of the jungle and know that you are on the road to understanding what you are buying.

The purpose of this book is to help you get out of the jungle and make your experience of working with creative service suppliers easier. This will be accomplished by educating you on all of the pieces that make up the whole.

By the time you have finished the book and implemented the use of the forms and checklists, you will be on your way to setting meaningful budgets, comparing apples to apples when getting estimates, knowing what is realistic when scheduling projects, and feeling in control when supervising your suppliers. You will make cost-effective and knowledgeable buying decisions that definitely affect your company's bottom line. This could be your chance to be a hero!

Acknowledgments

I would like to thank the people who have encouraged me and assisted me in putting this book together. Without their support and valuable input of information the book would still be an idea on a shelf. Specifically, to Vern Vihlene, Jr., Vihlene & Associates, Laguna Niguel, California, for endless hours of sharing his many years of expertise in the video production business; to Fred Martin, Frederick Martin & Company, Newport Beach, California, for his assistance and guidance as a great copywriter, in helping to lay the groundwork for this effort; and to Sue Seamon of Printronics, Inc., Irvine, California, whose insight as manager of advertising and promotions was invaluable. In addition, very special thanks to my editor, Richard Hagle, who continually, and with great patience, encouraged me and caused me to believe that a graphic artist can, indeed, write a book.

It would take too much space to thank all of the others by name in my industry for allowing me to interview them and ask endless questions. Also, special thanks to the PIA (Printing Industry of America) for permission to use their customs.

Finally, my warmest love and thanks to my children, Mark and Aimey, for their support and patience during my literary absence.

CHAPTER 1

The Name of the Game

"John, why is this bill for $1,500 more than we budgeted for this brochure?" asked the president of the company.

"Well, it's really rather embarrassing. I thought I could save us some money, so I selected the photographer with the lowest bid to shoot our new line of chrome wheels. I guess he didn't realize that the reflection of his assistant would show up in all the photos."

"But that doesn't explain the extra cost," replied the president.

"Oh, yes it does. It cost an additional $1,500 to retouch out the reflection."

"But, John, we shouldn't have to pay for that."

"That's true. But all the photographer offered to do is reshoot, and we didn't have time for that. So there was no choice but to retouch the shots."

I certainly hope you are getting the photographer to pay for that."

"Well," John replied, "that is actually being disputed right now. He claims his offer to reshoot was enough. Of course, I don't agree."

"You did have that type of thing covered in a written agreement before you started, didn't you?" asked the president. "Oh my gosh! By the look on your face, I think I know the answer."

Sound familiar? This kind of problem is repeated every day by all sorts of people at all levels of responsibility. Depending on the circles you travel in, you probably have heard one or more of the following:

- It could be the story about the designer who failed to tell his client that the "little logo" he wanted thrown in cost an extra $2,000.
- Or it could be the one about the "full service" shop that spent a client's entire budget on just the design of an ad.
- Or it could be the one about the producer whose verbal estimate of the cost of studio time for editing the client's corporate video was understated by 50 percent.

The stories—about overcharges, missed budgets, blown budgets, ineffective and inappropriate marketing pieces—are never-ending.

Working with people who offer creative services can be confusing, frustrating, and exhilarating—all at the same time. And that is exactly why this book is so important. Some people have had such bad experiences working with creative people that they hope never to do it again.

But many others regard their creative resources as an indispensable part of their marketing team. They know that they can trust these deadlines and provide top quality. They also know that when problems arise, they can count on their creative resources to handle the problems in stride—and help save the day.

The key differences between these two groups are understanding and experience. A clear understanding of the processes involved in producing marketing communications tools makes your job much easier. You don't have to be afraid of working with "those people." Once you develop the understanding of what you are buying, most aspects of working with providers of creative services can be done in a very practical manner. Even subjective evaluations and aesthetic judgments won't seem so difficult.

This book will help provide that understanding. It will guide you in defining your needs, selecting and communicating with suppliers, determining and managing a budget wisely, scheduling projects realistically, and working intelligently with production experts.

This is not a book on how to write a marketing plan or how to create effective advertising. It doesn't cover television, radio, or such exotica as global satellite communications and convention entertainment. It does, however, give you the practical guidance necessary to use the basic tools and processes involved in buying the right talent for creating and producing effective print materials and videos for your marketing efforts.

Before becoming involved in all the "how-to's" needed to work effectively with creative resources, let's take a look at some examples of who they are and what they do.

Key Marketing Tools

All forms of printed material, from matchbook covers to ad campaigns, are forms of marketing tools. Every time an organization's name or product appears in print or on the screen, it serves as a reminder of its existence; thus, it is a marketing tool. And all marketing tools require some form of the creative process to be produced.

For example, although it may appear that producing a flyer for a small business is very different from producing an ad for a large company, both tasks are very similar when it comes to the production process. They both need someone to come up with the idea, someone to do the artwork or write the copy, and someone to do the production and printing. The critical difference between the two pieces will most likely be the budget and distribution, therefore affecting the type of piece that is produced.

The next time you are in a store or in your office, write down how many types of tools you can find. You may be amazed by the length of the list. And when you finish this book, you will discover how similar the production process is for each tool. The following is an abbreviated list of the types of marketing tools available:

- Corporate image/logos, letterheads, business cards, envelopes, and forms
- Brochures, direct mail, catalogs, and annual reports
- Advertisements
- Sales or data sheets
- Newsletters
- Specialty advertising items (sometimes known as "trinkets and trash")

- Packaging (on-shelf and shipping)
- Posters and signage
- Point of purchase
- Audiovisual presentations and videos

Key Suppliers

Next, it is important to know the suppliers that are available and the tasks they perform. Detailed explanations of each task are provided in subsequent chapters of this book. But first you need to know what resources are available.

Creative Resources

- Graphic design studios
- Advertising agencies
- Marketing firms
- Copywriters
- Public relations agencies
- Video and film directors

Miscellaneous Resources

- Media buying services (print, television, and radio)
- Production companies (slide, video, television, radio, or multimedia)
- Marketing research companies
- Special event marketing individuals or companies
- Direct mail companies
- Packaging and container companies
- Exhibit and display companies

Production Resources

- Photographers
- Illustrators
- Talent (models and actors)
- Location search companies
- Food and makeup stylists
- Pre-press suppliers
- Printers
- Binderies
- Laminators

Be aware that it is just as easy to select the right supplier as the wrong one, and that your selection can make or break the project.

Once you are aware of the players and their contribution to the process, it will be easier to assign tasks and make decisions about scheduling, budgeting, and production. The nice part about this business is that there are some very highly trained professionals waiting to help you. You don't have to feel that if you don't do it yourself, it won't get done.

In fact, there are some things that you shouldn't even consider doing yourself. For instance, you may be able to do your own taxes, but have you ever tried to script a video so that it times at exactly five minutes, or have you ever operated a printing press? The best advice is: If you weren't trained to do it, don't do it.

By selecting the right team of suppliers, all you should need to do is be a good manager. You will be there to provide information, make decisions about quantity and deadlines, approve creative ideas and the elements that make up the final piece, and motivate the team.

You shouldn't need to pop aspirin and antacid tablets at every stage of the process. If you do, you have chosen the wrong team.

CHAPTER 2

Getting Started

Define the Problem

The process of buying creative services to produce a marketing or communications tool can be very simple or extremely complex. In either case, in order to do the job successfully, it is important to thoroughly understand every aspect of the process and who will perform each task. However, before you can explain your company's project to an outsider or become involved in its production, you have to know exactly what the project is yourself. You also need to know that you are, in fact, assigning the correct project to the correct suppliers.

Since every marketing or communications tool has a mission in life, it is a good idea to start by asking yourself, "What's the real reason this piece is needed?" Then, once you know the answer, your job will be easier.

You need to know certain information before you can decide on the communications tool you will need. The one thing you don't want to do is solve the wrong problem or solve the right problem with the wrong solution.

Consider the man who walks into a hardware store and asks for a drill. Does he really want a drill? Of course not. All he wants to do is to put a hole in something. If your fabric store is running a two-day special on a closeout item, would you spend the money for an ad in a national monthly publication? Of course not. It's really quite simple—find the right solution for the right problem.

Let's examine an example of a worst-case scenario, the wrong answer for the wrong problem. The ABC Manufacturing Company had lost a big chunk of market share to its competitors and was desperately seeking to turn itself around. A marketing firm proposed a research program to the executives of ABC, the results of which would form the basis for a comprehensive marketing plan. This plan would enable the company to define its problems and lead it to the road to recovery.

"But what color are we going to paint the trucks?" a senior executive kept asking. Finally, an even more senior executive said sternly, "Ben, if we don't properly define our problems now, we won't have any trucks to paint!"

So don't be afraid to take a closer look at what you are trying to accomplish. Whatever you do, don't move ahead until you have clearly defined the problem and are sure of the appropriate solution. You should feel comfortable that you are about to spend money on producing the correct tool.

There are many sources of valuable information available on marketing. This book is not intended to be a guide to writing your marketing plan. However, the following checklists will help provide the correct information to determine what marketing or communications tool is the best once your plan is in place. Some of the many marketing tools that can be utilized were listed in Chapter 1. Now you can decide which ones are right for you.

Even if yours is a very small business with a very limited budget, completing the tasks in Checklist 1 is necessary before you can move forward. In fact, when your budget is very limited, it is even more important to know that you have closely examined your marketing data. If you only have enough money for one shot out of the bag, you better make it a good one.

Too often, small businesses use their entire budget on one avenue of marketing for reasons that have nothing to do with sound marketing information. They may rely on something that worked for them in a different business, or they may have trusted a very effective salesperson who convinced them to take the wrong course of action. Whatever the reason, they discover the mistake too late to change gears. Then they feel frustrated because they do not have the budget to do anything else. Imagine the consequences of doing this on an even larger scale.

Like small businesses, nonprofit organizations should also spend time reviewing their goals and strategies before getting started. Conducting fund-raising efforts is no different in philosophy from marketing products or services for profit. There is a target audience that can be determined and the goal is to "sell" the target on supporting the organization. Whether the piece to be created is merely a party invitation or a set of informative material for a fund-raising campaign, it should be designed to meet the goals you have established and appeal to the market your organization has defined.

Checklist 1. Preliminary Information Gathering

Establish the objectives and goals of the project:

☐ Determine the plan to position your company to serve the needs of the market.

☐ Clearly define the market you plan to target.

☐ Determine how much of the potential market your company can realistically serve.

☐ Determine what the competition is doing.

☐ Review the company's specific goals for the next year and evaluate how you can meet them.

Understand the company's product mix:

☐ Determine the key products or services offered.

☐ Determine which products or services will produce the greatest profitability.

☐ Determine which products or services require a long-term sales effort.

☐ Evaluate the strength of the product by itself, as well as coupled with another product or service you offer.

Understand the company's promotional strategy:

☐ Determine if you will use existing or new channels of product distribution.

☐ Determine the image that should be projected.

☐ Determine the major goal of the marketing efforts in terms of potential revenue that can be generated. Later, quantify the results by comparing the percentage of the budget that was spent to meet your projections.

☐ Evaluate the available media and determine which form(s) will be used.

☐ Review every possible way that the customer can be sold and other promotional strategies that will be used to support the marketing efforts.

☐ Establish an integrated direction for marketing to the trade as well as the consumer.

If your company has the budget to hire a market research firm, it is a worthwhile investment to use it to help you determine the demographics, psychographics, or location of your potential customers. If you are operating on a limited budget, try to gather as much of this information as possible. The following are some of the resources available to help you do your research:

- Trade organizations
- College or public libraries
- On-line database services
- One-on-one interviews with experts in your field (even the competition)
- Media demographics (Most publications have information available about the market they serve.)
- Focus group studies with potential customers to determine receptivity of the product or service

However you are able to gather the information, prior to making any final decisions about how to reach your target market, learn as much as possible about your targeted audience. The information in Checklist 1 can be helpful only if it reflects an in-depth review of the available market data.

Many large companies spend millions of dollars on market research before making decisions on how to correctly market a product or service. They spend a great deal of time selecting professionals they can trust to do the research and develop programs that reflect the correct marketing strategy.

Still, in spite of all the money spent on advertising and marketing campaigns, sometimes products or services simply don't sell. The problem could be the marketing technique, bad timing, or the product itself. It can happen to anybody. This fact of life is not much of a confidence builder if you are about to invest in producing the tools for a marketing campaign and you want to have faith in your purchasing decisions. Nevertheless, it shouldn't prevent you from doing the research or following through with the campaign. It simply means that you should prepare as much as you can so that you know that you did your very best to cover all the bases.

You may not be the actual person to determine the information in Checklist 1; however, your job will be a lot easier if you have the data in hand before you proceed. If the information is too difficult to determine, then do the best you can. Don't be afraid to ask your coworkers a lot of questions. Find out if the research has been done and what information is available to you. Ask the president or owner, your boss, department heads, technical or staff support, or anyone else who may know. You may want to go outside the company for some answers. Ask customers, suppliers, or even competitors. You may be surprised how willing people are to express their opinions or offer information.

Preliminary Organization

After you have completed Checklist 1, you will be ready to begin your planning on paper. Make a chart of the points that come up most often and with the most emphasis. Clear up any additional questions that may arise by going back to your sources and asking for clarification. List your determination of the objectives and goals as you see them, and make sure that you have defined the problem correctly. Review any obstacles that may impede success and find out what will be done to surmount them.

Now you are ready to present this information to your superiors (unless you are in charge!) and confirm that you are on the right track. If you aren't, either restate your case with more supportive research and evidence or reevaluate your definition of the problem by reexamining the information you have gathered.

Even if you have been given full reins to oversee a project, it is a good idea to make sure that there is a consensus among the management or key personnel regarding what you are trying to accomplish and how you will get there. If there is no consensus and no agreement is in sight, then find the person with the most authority and get the information in writing with a signature and date.

Would you want to be responsible for deciding to spend money for marketing materials for a business-to-business trade show booth only to find out too late that your boss only wanted to market to consumers directly in a national advertising campaign? Mistakes like that are a common result of miscommunication or, even worse, no communication. A dated signature will serve to protect you, as well as demonstrate your thoroughness. Because some of the decisions you will be making are subjective, the more hard data you have to support your decisions, the better off you will be.

With your checklist completed and your definition of the problem to be solved signed and in hand, you are ready to move forward and define the project.

CHAPTER 3

Defining the Project

When buying creative services, you will need to make many subjective evaluations and decisions. The work you did in the previous chapter prepared you to make those evaluations and decisions easier. Now you are ready to assess which tool works best to meet the marketing goals you outlined in Checklist 1. If you do not know how to do this, the following information will help.

Discover Which Tools Are the Best

Review the list of marketing tools in Chapter 1. Add any others to the list that you have identified. See if you feel comfortable choosing the tools to meet the objectives and goals you have defined. If you don't feel comfortable, follow the advice in the adage: "When in doubt, ask." So, if you have no experience on which to rely when choosing the right marketing tool, ask someone who does.

- Begin with someone else in your company who may have successfully completed a similar project.
- Contact a marketing professional who is familiar with your target market.
- Ask your creative professionals (i.e., ad agencies, designers, direct mail consultants, writers) for their recommendations.
- Ask your customers what they would respond to. (However, they are not always right!)
- Snoop around the competition. Find out what your competitors have done that worked or didn't work.

- Ask others in industries related to yours what they have done and what results they experienced.
- Use public or college libraries. (Reference librarians will often help you do the research.)
- Contact trade organization resource centers.

The bottom line is that if you are not hiring someone else to advise you, such as your ad agency or a professional consultant, then you need to research as much available data as possible on the effectiveness of different marketing programs.

Remember, there are many variables when assessing the success of utilizing any marketing tool. What worked for someone else does not guarantee that it will work for you. Any time you can get hard numbers and measured responses you will be better off. But hard data do not always account for unforeseen events that affect buyers' spending habits. Global economics, the weather, natural disasters, or bad timing can affect even the best strategies. Sometimes the success or failure of a marketing campaign has little to do with its effectiveness. In any event, trust the advice from someone who knows what he or she is talking about, rather than guessing.

Determining the correct tool, the correct quantity, and the right method of distribution is a little like knowing what food to serve at a dinner party. It takes a little planning. Whatever you do, don't "just throw the spaghetti against the wall to see what sticks." That approach can waste valuable time and money, not to mention the mess you have to clean up when you're done.

Beware of the Creative Crazies

Now it is time to contradict the entire concept of basing your decisions on what has worked in the past. Some of the most successful marketing has been innovative and sometimes a little crazy.

A customer of mine had tried everything to break into a new market for his product. After picking his brain, I discovered that he had never thought of selling first to the distributors. He adamantly insisted that they were very close-minded and impossible to penetrate. I convinced him that if we could get the trade excited, then it would be easier to get the consumer excited. So we sent out personalized items to each distributor with a series of customized, humorous greeting cards. Would you believe that the distributors actually started calling and asking for the next card and gift? By the time the campaign was over, my client had exceeded his dreams in setting up new distributors and selling his product.

If everyone else in your industry is doing ads, maybe you should do direct mail. If you can't afford to have a booth at the trade show, consider a hospitality suite, or buy the list of attendees and send them something unique to store all of their literature when the show is over. Maybe the solution is something as crazy as a trash can with your logo on it.

It is a little scary to be a trendsetter. Safe always feels better. But try stepping outside your box every so often and take a different look.

Be Smarter and Faster

Knowing which communications tools to produce does not automatically guarantee a competitive edge. The most creative, well-considered campaign will not be effective if it is not timely.

Several years ago a software company decided to conduct a very aggressive marketing campaign for its newest product. The company's decision-makers knew about the competition on the market, but they felt confident that their product was much stronger. They devoted a large portion of their budget to brochures, more space at their next trade show, and a direct mail campaign that followed the trade show.

It was a great concept. But, as a result of disorganization and procrastination, all of their efforts were ultimately directed toward releasing the marketing campaign at the show rather than before it. Everything was done at crisis speeds. Several mistakes appeared in the literature and, of course, there was no time or money to correct the mistakes.

Meanwhile, their biggest competition, a much smaller company with a weaker product, had selected a similar marketing strategy. However, it decided to team up with a hardware company to present a special offer. The hardware company also invested in the marketing campaign, therefore doubling the promotional budget. The campaign was very well organized and was released *before* the trade show, along with many press releases to the media. As a result of good planning, there was plenty of time to spark media interest in this unique partnership, and their campaign was very successful.

Needless to say, the other company was disappointed by the response at the trade show and to the direct mail campaign that followed. No one could understand why their similar campaign and superior product didn't do better than the competition.

What went wrong here? Simply, the second company was more creative with its budget and was able to get more mileage out of its dollars by teaming up with another company. More important, the second company's decision-makers planned ahead. This is not a new trick. It is just a good example of a company that was willing to look at options before getting started. They knew what they were trying to accomplish and determined a strong approach to doing so. In other words, they were smarter and faster.

Getting Ready

Whatever tool you decide to produce, you must be ready for your suppliers before turning anything over to them. Checklist 2 provides a list of the information you should have before beginning production of any project. Whether you will be working with a printer, a graphic designer, a copywriter, or an advertising agency, you need to be well prepared and gather as much information as possible.

It is your job to piece together all this information, or at the very least, know where to tell suppliers to find it. Clear communication of all the details of the project will help avoid costly mistakes or delays. In order to be clear to others, you need to begin by being clear to yourself and know *everything* about your project. If you do not provide all the necessary information, you will pay for someone else to find it later, one way or the other.

Checklist 2. Information Gathering

☐ What elements will be necessary to produce the project and who will provide them?

☐ What are the pieces that will be produced?

☐ How many of each piece will be produced?

☐ What is the deadline?

☐ What is the budget?

☐ Is the time frame realistic?

☐ What preexisting pieces can be provided (i.e., photos, illustrations, logos, charts or graphs, copy points)?

☐ What background information is available?

☐ Is there a format that needs to be followed? Is there a corporate manual of style?

☐ Who will be part of the approval process?

☐ Who is available for questions?

☐ Where will the job be delivered?

☐ Is the product or service ready to be released to the marketplace?

Although every one of these points is very important, none of the research and planning will be worthwhile if the last point is not resolved. One of the biggest public relations nightmares you can create is to sell and not be able to deliver.

The goal of any marketing tool is to communicate information. If the information is incorrect, you may have a problem with misrepresentation. However, this type of problem can be resolved by quickly notifying your public of the error and issuing an apology. Some feathers may be ruffled and you may even lose some business, but chances are you will recover. On the other hand, if you can't deliver what you are promising, you will definitely lose the business, as well as the money and time invested in the marketing campaign.

Many years ago my company was hired to help release a new product. We prepared an aggressive, award-winning campaign with three different full-page, full-color ads in national publications, a sales video, direct mail, brochures, data sheets, and public relations and sales training materials. The entire campaign came to a screeching halt after only two of the three ads ran.

The client had not anticipated the excellent results of the campaign and didn't want to invest in additional salespeople to respond to the numerous leads brought in through the ads. In addition, the product was not quite ready, and the shipping date of the final units kept being delayed. Potential customers lost interest because they were never contacted following their inquiries about the product. Distributors were upset because of the demand for a product that was not available. Certainly, this was a sad ending to what was about to become a success story.

Remember, your goal is to *manage* the creation and production of the marketing communications tools. A good manager is organized and provides clear instructions to all team members. But most important is the willingness and ability to troubleshoot potential obstacles, such as those in the preceding story.

There is one more reason you will want to pull together all the information mentioned up to this point. You will need it in the chapters ahead, when you start putting together a budget, a schedule, and a creative team that can get the job done for you—on time, on target, and on budget. You will be on your way to becoming that corporate hero.

CHAPTER 4

Scheduling

"In the building of a creative product, you can get it good, you can get it fast, and you can get it cheap. You may take your choice of any two, but it is God's truth that you cannot have all three together." Those are indeed words to live by.

The business world is filled with legends of remarkable turnarounds: new products rushed to market in a month, from conception to production; advertising campaigns created and produced in a week; and brochures cranked out in days. But the truth is, in virtually every case, something had to give. To beat an awesome deadline, either quality or budget can be greatly affected—and sometimes both suffer.

When creating a schedule, two factors of quality and deadline need to be considered. If you have a rush deadline, you may need to forsake quality. Ask your suppliers what is realistic for the quality you want. Keep in mind the capability of your supplier and the complexity of the project. You may need to pay a little more to find suppliers that can meet your quality and schedule demands.

Planning for Pitfalls

When scheduling a project with a tight deadline, allow for every factor that may affect production, including mechanical or technological breakdowns! Although maintenance is important to most suppliers, we all know that technology-based equipment sometimes has a mind of its own.

If you are the slightest bit nervous about meeting a tight deadline, discuss with your supplier alternative solutions to hypothetical delays.

Do not move forward until you are confident that nothing will stand in the way of your deadline, not even a snowstorm, a sick art director, or an absentee boss.

Most often than not, slowdowns happen on the client side. Art boards and proofs have sat on many desks waiting for approval. If the person with the final approval power will not be available during the course of the project, either find a different person with approval authority or change the schedule. You may have to bring in some hard proof of the potential consequences to support those necessary changes, but it will be worth it.

The best schedules have been destroyed by disorganization and miscommunication. Before any work begins, make sure that both the product and you are ready. Many of your suppliers will be paid by the hour. It is not cost-effective to have them sit around while on the clock because you were not prepared.

The following scheduling nightmare helped me demonstrate to a client just how important it is to be prepared: We hired a photographer, a model, and a makeup stylist, and we rented props for a simple morning photo shoot of a computer. When it was time to shoot, we discovered that the wrong program had been installed in the computer. After waiting three hours for the technician to return with the correct software, he announced that it had a bug and that the corrected version would not be available for two weeks. Worse yet, the computer, the only existing prototype, was needed at a trade show about the time the software would be ready.

We ultimately rehired the crew and shot three weeks later. Not only did the client have to pay everybody involved for twice as much time, but also the schedule delay caused the client to miss an ad deadline for a publication. How simple it would have been to check the computer *before* it left the warehouse!

Figure 4.1 shows the time it should take to produce some typical projects. Keep in mind that meeting specific schedules requires everyone's cooperation and readiness. Some tasks can overlap while others need to be done consecutively. Through good planning you can avoid costly errors caused by rushing and lack of organization.

Figure 4.1 Production Schedules

The following examples are best-case scenarios based on artwork prepared on the computer with film produced directly from the computer file. If the artwork is done on art boards, add two to four days for making camera work and stripping, two days for typesetting, two days for typesetting revisions, and two to four days for paste-ups (depending on the size of the project). Some of the tasks can be done at the same time to expedite the process (e.g., specifications to the printer while mechanical artwork is being prepared).

Stationery Package *(4 to 5 weeks)*—Includes the production of a logo and its application in two colors with blind embossing of letterheads, envelopes, and business cards.
Note: Extra time is required for embossing. If the logo art is not complicated to produce or if there is no logo art, the artwork could be done in less time.

Design (Includes revised layout)	1 to 2 weeks
Client approval	2 days
Quotations from printers	2 days
Selection of printer	1 day
Mechanical art	1 week
Proofreading of mechanicals or laser proofs	1 day
Film output and stripping	2 days
Preparation of blueline proofs	1 day
Client approval of bluelines	1 day
Plate and die-making	3 days
Printing/embossing	3 days
Bindery (trimming and packaging)	1 day

Eight-Page Brochure *(7 to 8 weeks)*—Includes the design and production of a four-color premium quality brochure with eight photographs and no illustrations. Quantity: 25,000.

Initial layouts	1 week
Copywriting	1 week

Figure 4.1   Production Schedules *(continued)*

Client approval	1 day
Final layouts and copy	3 days
Client approval	1 day
Quotations from printers	3 days
Photography and film processing	3 days
Selection of printer	1 day
Sizing and scanning of photos	3 days
Preparation of mechanical art	1 week
Proofreading of mechanicals or laser proofs	1 day
Correction of mechanicals	2 days
Production of film	3 days
Review of color proofs and bluelines	1 day
Correction of color	2 days
Platemaking	1 day
Printing	2 days
Bindery	1 day
Delivery (local)	1 day

Five- to Seven-Minute Video *(6 to 7 weeks)*—This schedule can vary from six weeks to as long as three months, depending on the amount of client revisions to the script and off-line editing.

Creative and storyboards	1 week
Script	1 week (to 2 months)
Pre-production	2 weeks
Shooting	1 to 5 days
Off-line editing	1 day to 1 month
On-line editing and delivery	1 day to 1 week
Mass duplication	1 week

In addition to the general time lines in Figure 4.1, there are some simple rules to follow when setting your production schedule. The following checklist will keep your expectations on track with reality. If you need to explain to the higher-ups why you must change either a deadline or the scope of the project, it will be much easier if you have done your work ahead of time.

Checklist 3. Setting a Schedule

☐ What is the very latest, realistic deadline that will be acceptable?

☐ Is all the information required to do the project ready to be handed over to the creative team?

☐ Have all aspects of the production process been included?

☐ Did you allow ample time for the approval cycle and revisions?

☐ Will key personnel be available for the approval process?

☐ Is the product ready for photography?

☐ Will the product be ready for distribution when the marketing campaign breaks?

☐ Did you allow for shipping?

☐ Can your suppliers meet your deadline while maintaining your expectations of quality?

☐ Are your suppliers available?

Establishing an Erg List

Probably the best advice that can be given about scheduling is to tell you where to start: at the end. At this point, the most useful task is the creation of an erg list. (For those of you who are not crossword-puzzle fans, an *erg* is a unit of work.) List each erg for the project, working backward. That way you leave nothing out. Once you put all of those little ergs on a piece of paper, you will realize what a complex thing your project is—how many people and steps and professional decisions it involves.

Figure 4.2 is a sample "erg list" established to determine who does what. We will assume that you have already selected your creative team—an ad agency, design group, or freelance team—to do the actual work for you. You will see that what may appear on the surface to be a simple little project may involve as many as forty tasks. And that doesn't include the behind-the-scenes tasks that you don't need to worry about.

Getting Out the Calendar

Next, set your target finish date and establish a time frame for each specific erg. Now you really need to start at the end, because your suppliers can greatly affect your plans. It would be a shame to finish all the work only to find there is no way in the world the printer—any printer—can get the job done by the time you need it. You may want to confirm with your suppliers that you haven't created a monster and allowed too little time for each task.

If you truly want quality, especially at the creative end, allow for the time it takes. Remember, the more time your creative team has to seek the "golden snowflake," the better the chances that it will find it for you.

Now you can go back to the beginning. With your erg list in hand and target date set, sit down with the calendar. After you have resolved both ends of the schedule, the rest is easy. Fill in the middle until everything is covered and the schedule works to fit the time available for the project.

A word of caution. Don't cheat. Many items on your long list may appear to be unimportant or to take very little time. You may be tempted to eliminate one of them to expedite the process. But all items are included because even the smallest tasks need to be accommodated. Some tasks can be done concurrently, but don't remove anything from the list unless you are absolutely sure it is not going to haunt you later.

To coin a phrase, hope for the best and schedule for the worst. Do that and you'll come as close as humanly possible to getting it done "good, fast, and cheap."

Figure 4.2   Sample Erg List for a Brochure

The following is a hypothetical list for a twelve-page, four-color brochure with photographs and illustrations. It is based on the assumption that you have already selected the suppliers. If you have not done so, add the selection process to the list. Some of the tasks can be done at the same time. The ideal production time for this project, from creative concept to delivery, would be eight to ten weeks. Client preparation time would be additional. Task assignments for other projects vary, based on the scope of the project.

Unit of Work (Erg)	Who Does It?*	How Long?
Define problem	Me*	1 day
Establish budget	Me	2 days
Brief internal staff	Me	1 day
Redefine problem	Management	2 days
Secure bids from suppliers	Me	4 days
Redefine budget with estimates	Me	1 day
Discuss redefined problem	Us	1 day
Review redefined budget	Us	1 day
Approve budget	Management	2 days
Develop preliminary schedule	Management	1 day
Gather preliminary information	Me	5 days
Brief creative team	Me	1 day
Develop creative approaches	Creative team	2 weeks
Review creative approaches	Us	3 days
Select best creative approach	Us	1 day
Layouts	Designer or art director	1 day
Copywriting	Copywriter	2 weeks
Review layout and copy	Us	3 days
Revise layout and copy	Artist and writer	3 days
Secure company approvals	Me	3 days
Secure product for photography	Me	2 days
Hire photographer	Designer or agency	1 day
Hire makeup stylist	Photographer	15 minutes
Hire or secure models	Agency	1 week
Secure scenic locations	Designer or agency	3–4 days

*Note: Me = you, the client, and Us = you and your staff or management.

Figure 4.2   Sample Erg List for a Brochure _(continued)_

Unit of Work (Erg)	Who Does It?*	How Long?
Secure facility locations	Me	1–2 days
Schedule photography	Me	15 minutes
Take pictures, process film	Photographer	4 days
Art direct photography	Designer or art director	2 days
Review photographs	Designer or art director and us	1 day
Select photographs	Designer or art director and us	1 day
Final layout and copy revision	Artist and writer	3 days
Final layout and copy approval	Us	2 days
Select printer	Designer or agency	1 day
Reserve press time	Designer or agency	15 minutes
Prepare illustrations	Illustrator or designer	2 weeks
Input final copy for artwork or typesetting	Designer or agency	2 days
Prepare camera-ready art	Designer or agency	1 week
Read proofs of artwork	Us	3 days
Revisions of artwork	Designer or agency	3 days
Final approval of artwork	Me	1 day
Deliver all materials to printer	Designer or agency	1 day
Scan photos and prepare film	Printer	5 days
Check preliminary color proofs of photos	Designer or agency	1 day
Correct color	Printer	2 days
Approve final color	Me	1 day
Make bluelines and composed color proof	Printer	2 days
Read bluelines and color proofs twelve times	Us	3 days
Sign bluelines and color proofs	Me (gulp)	1 day
Check press proofs	Designer or agency and me	2 days
Approve press proofs	Designer or agency and me	1 day
Bindery	Printer	3 days
Shipping	Printer	4 days

CHAPTER 5

Setting a Budget

The task of setting a budget or schedule for any project never seems to be one that is met with open arms. It is rare indeed to hear those wonderful words, "The sky is the limit, I want the best and I don't care what it costs or how long it takes." More common is the situation of "champagne tastes on a beer budget" and no time to get it done.

I hope you have done the work in the previous chapters. If you did, you should have a very good idea of what you are trying to accomplish and how you will achieve it. If you didn't, return to "go" and start again. After all, how will you ever know what something will cost or how long it will take to produce if you don't even know what it is? Have you ever tried to establish the cost of a party before deciding what type of party it will be, how many people will attend, or what you will serve? It's pretty tough, isn't it?

Good planning and organization are the key to controlling your projects. In this chapter you will learn how to establish budgets. This chapter focuses on the business aspects of managing a project, and subsequent chapters will cover the technical aspects of producing the project.

Ultimately, you will see how much the business part of the process will be affected by the hundreds of variables of the technical part. But even before taking into account all the technical considerations, setting up the framework of your project and setting a budget and schedule will be the most important steps in effective management.

Preliminary Steps for Setting a Budget

Before you can do a budget—whether it's for an annual report, a special project, or even for running the government of the United States—you really must know what you are dealing with. As an aid to planning, you will need a Job Organizer (Figure 5.1) to identify all the tasks that need to be done, who will do them, and eventually what they will cost.

Each unit of work has dozens of little units of work that must be performed by someone—thus they have a cost attached. Remember the erg list you created in Chapter 4. It's time to get it out and dust it off. If your project has several parts, you may need to use more than one list. For example, if you are producing a video, brochures, and an ad campaign, each may require different types of tasks and certainly a variety of different suppliers to do them. Therefore, it will be easier to break down the overall project into parts, each with its own budget and schedule. Then it will be easier later to analyze how they interrelate and to establish an overview of the components as one large project.

If your budget is preliminary, reorganize your erg lists into categories, rather than tasks. That way you can assign an overall number to each category and not become bogged down by individual costs. If you discover that you can't determine your preliminary budget without more detail, then you may need to assign some hypothetical numbers to each task.

There are several ways to gather preliminary information when establishing a budget. Again, you may need to do a little research. The steps you needed to take in defining the project will help you here as a good place to start.

Those with experience will know that the more information that is available the easier the task of setting a budget. However, sometimes it happens that you just aren't sure what you may be producing, nor do you know the details of what will make it happen. So be ready again to ask many questions and work with people who can give you a kick start. Checklist 4 provides some suggestions to help you set a *preliminary* budget.

Figure 5.1   Job Organizer

Project: _____

Project Number: _____

Before you fill in the chart, note that not all tasks will have a cost and not all tasks may be required. Fill in the applicable information only.

Task	Cost Estimate	Due Date	Person/Company Responsible
Creative Development:			
Initial meeting with designer/agency	_____	_____	_____
Contact subs/vendors	_____	_____	_____
Project estimate	_____	_____	_____
Information gathering	_____	_____	_____
Information to designer/agency	_____	_____	_____
Information to copywriter	_____	_____	_____
Concept and initial layout	_____	_____	_____
Script treatment	_____	_____	_____
Copy	_____	_____	_____
Script	_____	_____	_____
Client approval of initial concept	_____	_____	_____
Copy revisions	_____	_____	_____
Final approval of copy	_____	_____	_____
Final layout	_____	_____	_____
Client approval	_____	_____	_____

Figure 5.1   Job Organizer _(continued)_

Task	Cost Estimate	Due Date	Person/Company Responsible
Comprehensive layout	_____	_____	_____
Client approval	_____	_____	_____
Production:			
Photography	_____	_____	_____
Illustration	_____	_____	_____
Mechanical artwork	_____	_____	_____
Artwork revisions	_____	_____	_____
Artwork final approval	_____	_____	_____
Pre-press:			
Artwork to service bureau or printer	_____	_____	_____
Bluelines/color proofs	_____	_____	_____
Revisions	_____	_____	_____
Client approval	_____	_____	_____
Film to printer (or to platemaking	_____	_____	_____
Printing:			
Press check	_____	_____	_____
Printing to bindery	_____	_____	_____
Delivery	_____	_____	_____
Video Production:			
Pre-production	_____	_____	_____
Shoot	_____	_____	_____
Post-production	_____	_____	_____
Delivery	_____	_____	_____

Checklist 4. Setting a Preliminary Budget

☐ What are the costs of previous similar projects that you or someone in your company has done? Take into consideration how long ago the projects were done; costs often change dramatically.

☐ What are the estimates from suppliers based on samples from projects that already exist? It doesn't matter whether the samples are from something you did or someone else did. If you don't have samples, what exactly are you looking for? Make a list or use a "Request for Preliminary Estimate" form (Figure 5.2).

☐ Does an established budget already exist? A budget for your project may be part of a marketing figure but not broken out as a line item, or it might be part of some other budget that you never expected (e.g., the training or communications budget instead of the marketing budget). You may have to do some snooping.

☐ Can your creative resources help develop the budget with you?

☐ How much is the project worth to you? Would you spend $10,000 to promote a product that could earn you a profit of only $5,000 from the promotion?)

Preliminary vs. Final Budget

Remember, at this point you have only established a preliminary budget. Preliminary and final budgets can be quite different. In the beginning you may have no idea of what you really want. In that case, you may choose to authorize an amount for your creative resources to do a certain amount of creative development. Give them a hint, if you can, of how much is in the overall budget. They can then come up with ideas, each with a price tag.

The overall budget may be preliminary. The numbers assigned to producing an actual idea should be the final budget. These numbers should not be guesstimates but real figures. When those numbers start filling in the empty spaces in the working budget, some maneuvering may be necessary based on the idea you choose to use. However, when all the actual numbers appear on paper and you have decided what you want, you will have a final budget.

A quick caution about setting up the budget for work done in-house: when preparing the budget, make sure to include all costs, such as overhead, supplies, or any other production costs. Don't forget to include the cost of your own involvement, especially if it takes you away from other billable time.

Soliciting Quotations

It would be ideal to rely on your creative people to provide production cost estimates rather than soliciting them yourself. After all, they do this every day and you may not. If you are the chosen one, however, be very clear in the information you provide the suppliers and make sure you really understand the project and how it needs to be produced. Use a "Request for Quotation" form (Figure 5.4.) Fill it out as completely as possible and provide the *same* information to each competing supplier. If you are asking your suppliers for suggestions, then give all the suppliers the same information.

By the time you complete this book, the language your suppliers speak will not seem foreign, and you will be able to solicit bids with ease. Filling out the forms will be a welcome task, rather than a frightening obstacle. The biggest communication breakdowns usually happen at this level, right at the beginning. If you know what you are buying and you and the supplier agree on the work to be provided, there should be no problems.

If the Request for Quotation form is incomplete or erroneous, you could be in trouble. *Never* allow for assumptions. Even if you aren't sure about certain specifics, at least come as close as possible. A hypothetical yet detailed scenario is far better than an actual but vague one.

As mentioned earlier, budgets can be affected by many variables. Because of this, decisions need to be made up front about quality, image, function, and schedule. After those decisions are made, you are ready to identify a list of suppliers that will meet your criteria. Then you can make valid evaluations and comparisons.

If you are selecting a creative team for future projects rather than suppliers for specific projects (e.g., selecting your ad agency for the next year or a video company for a series of projects), it is more difficult to solicit exact quotations. However, you can ask potential suppliers to

Figure 5.2 Request for Preliminary Estimates

Please fill out completely. Use a different form for each project.

Company: _____

Contact person: _____

Address: _____

Phone: _____ Ext.: _____ Date: _____

Project description: _____

_____

_____

_____

Project Management Costs:

    Research   _____

    Meetings and coordination   _____

Creative Costs:

    Concept and layout   _____

    Production art   _____

    Copywriting   _____

    Art direction   _____

    Illustration   _____

          Subtotal   _____

Supplier Costs *(fill out the applicable information only):*

    Photography   _____

      Film and processing   _____

      Props   _____

      Stylist   _____

Figure 5.2   Request for Preliminary Estimates *(continued)*

Typesetting   _____

Computer output (to paper)   _____

Pre-press   _____

Printing *(use one cost only in subtotal)*

     Quantity 1   _____

     Quantity 2   _____   _____

     Quantity 3   _____   _____

         Subtotal   _____

Miscellaneous costs:

     Travel *(explain)* _____

     _____   _____

     Copies   _____

     Delivery   _____

     Cartage   _____

     Other *(explain)* _____

     _____   _____

Subtotal   _____

Taxable total   _____

Sales tax   _____

TOTAL   _____

Figure 5.3   Request for Proposal

Name: _____

Company: _____

Address: _____

Phone: _____ Ext.: _____ Date: _____

Description of company services or products: _____

_____

_____

_____

Project title: _____

Project description: _____

   Item 1 _____

   Item 2 _____

   Item 3 _____

Proposal due date: _____

Project due date: Item 1 _____ Item 2 _____ Item 3 _____

Overall budget: _____

Number of copies
   (or desired length): Item 1 _____ Item 2 _____ Item 3 _____

Level of quality: basic _____ good _____ best _____ superior _____

Description of tasks to be provided by supplier (e.g., photography, design, copywriting, printing, etc.: _____

_____

_____

_____

_____

Figure 5.4   Request for Quotation

Please fill out completely. Use a different form for each project.

Company: _____

Contact person: _____

Address: _____

Phone: _____ Ext.: _____ Date: _____

Project description: _____

_____

_____

_____

Project Management Costs:

Research   _____

Meetings and coordination   _____

Creative Costs:

Concept and layout   _____

Production art   _____

Copywriting   _____

Art direction   _____

Illustration   _____

Subtotal   _____

Supplier Costs *(fill out the applicable information only):*

Photography   _____

Film and processing   _____

Props   _____

Stylist   _____

(continued)

Figure 5.4 Request for Quotation *(continued)*

Typesetting   _____

Computer output (to paper)   _____

Pre-press   _____

Printing *(use one cost only in subtotal)*

   Quantity 1   _____

   Quantity 2   _____

   Quantity 3   _____

   Subtotal   _____

Miscellaneous costs:

   Travel *(explain)* _____

   _____   _____

   Copies   _____

   Delivery   _____

   Cartage   _____

   Other *(explain)* _____

   _____   _____

Subtotal   _____

Taxable total   _____

Sales tax   _____

TOTAL   _____ provide cost estimates using hypothetical scenarios or to share how much it cost to produce a project they have already completed. Some firms even charge a consulting fee when asked to make suggestions on how they would spend your long-term budget.

Although some suppliers may not charge you to do this, keep in mind that analyzing how to spend a budget is actually part of designing a marketing plan, especially if it is for a long period of time or for something that might require complex planning. Some consultants make a living helping their clients with this type of planning. Others include it in the proposal as part of their efforts to be included in the bigger picture.

Evaluating Estimates

There is more to selecting a supplier than looking at the numbers. There are several "danger zones" that can fool even the most astute buyers. I have seen quotes presented in many forms, from scribbles on napkins to elaborate, formal proposals. It doesn't mean that the supplier with the napkin letterhead isn't capable, but it does leave too much open. On the other hand, beware of the fine print. Details should never be overlooked. It is Murphy's Law that the area of the proposal that you didn't read will be the one that surfaces later in a dispute. Checklist 5 provides an overview of things to look for when comparing estimates.

Checklist 5. Comparing Quotations

- ☐ Is the description of the scope of work identical for each supplier that is bidding on the project?
- ☐ Do the competing suppliers do similar work on a regular basis?
- ☐ Is every specification that you provided covered in each supplier's estimate?
- ☐ What will the delivery schedule be?
- ☐ What are the terms of payment?
- ☐ Who will actually be doing the work? Will the final work be done by the staff designated in the proposal?

☐ Will any of the work be subcontracted by the supplier? If so, are you pleased with the subcontractors?

☐ What is the reputation of the supplier?

☐ How long is the estimate valid?

☐ What are the possible add-on costs that may not appear in the original quotation (for example, props, film processing, proofs, shipping, rush charges, travel expenses, paper cost increases, or other additional production charges)?

☐ Who owns the artwork, photography, or slides (or in the case of video, the original film) once the project is completed? If ownership is not included, what will future usage fees be?

☐ How much will additional copies cost in the future?

☐ How are revision costs billed?

If these questions are asked early on, horror stories will diminish greatly. Let me share a story with you that will illustrate this point.

I recently was brought into a project to save a sinking ship. My client decided to produce his own artwork for his 200-page catalog. His nightmare started when he found out that the copy was typed by his free-lance writer into a very old computer program. His work could not easily be imported into a current desktop publishing program that is used to produce artwork for brochures or catalogs.

Furthermore, the client mistakenly thought that the program *was* a desktop publishing program that included graphics capabilities. He was surprised to hear that he couldn't just scan in his 600 photos, position the photos on the pages, and send them to the printer. Not only did he have the wrong computer program, but also he didn't even have a computer that was set up for this type of project.

Meanwhile, he had been getting bids from printers, giving each of them different information. One printer provided a cost based on printing only, not including the film required to make the printing plates. He assumed the client would take care of that part. Another printer provided a cost for creating new artwork on the computer, scanning the photos, creating the film, and printing the job. Others assumed that they would get old-fashioned *pasteups* from the client, and they included shooting the photographs as opposed to scanning them (see Chapter 10) and *stripping* them in by hand rather than doing it all on the computer. To add to the confusion, each printer based its cost on using a different paper. To top it off, the printers all specialized in different types of printing and had very different types of equipment.

It was no surprise at all that the differences in prices ranged $25,000 for only 2,500 copies. After you read the technical portion of this book, you will see that this was definitely a case of comparing apples to tangerines.

Our first step was to find a way to save the work that had been done, then to make sure that every printer was asked to bid on the same work, done the same way, on the same paper. By doing so, my client's estimates dropped by more than 50 percent below the prior lowest bid, and most of the new estimates were within $1,500 of each other. Not too bad on a $40,000 job.

Know What You Are Buying

Don't be surprised if your final estimates don't match your original budget. It happens all the time. You may end up with the cost of a diamond when you thought you were buying cut glass.

Of course, it is always possible to find someone who will do the job for less. Just make sure that you know what you will be getting—after all, there really is no such thing as a "free lunch." You may end up compromising your standards for the sake of the budget. It may be better to rethink the project. Maybe your four-color, twelve-page brochure might end up as a two-color, eight-pager, or your dynamic, thirty-minute video will become a slide show.

You have now reached the stage where you have reviewed all the submissions and have selected the ones that meet your goals—budget and otherwise. Now, make sure to review and sign the final quotations of those you will be using. Your final quotation will be a reference for making sure all the work was completed according to the specifications. Unless revisions are made, the final bill should match or come fairly close to the quotation. If revisions are necessary, ask for a written quotation of costs and sign it before allowing the work to proceed. Do not be taken by surprise when the suppliers' invoices arrive.

CHAPTER 6

Selecting the Right Suppliers

Be forewarned. There is no scientific, guaranteed way to select the right suppliers. Choosing a creative resource is different from choosing a lawyer or an accountant. The people you will be dealing with are significantly different from lawyers and accountants. Creatives (a popular term for "creative people/resources") talk differently, think differently, and sometimes dress differently. More than anything else, the services they provide are completely different.

But here's the catch. Unless creatives are also solid, hard-nosed businesspeople, they will not last more than a few years in the competitive arena. They will, at best, be designing the classified ad pages for the local shopping news. The same is true for all the other related suppliers in the industry.

Selecting the appropriate creative resources for your project boils down to two main requirements: (1) the resource must be right for your project, and (2) the resource must be right for you. Remember those two requirements because we'll be coming back to them many times.

What Kind of Creative Resource?

The right one, of course. Your creative resource should fit you, your company, and the work you need done, and be one with which you can enjoy a long-term relationship. Repeatedly going after new resources is wasteful and more often reflects poorly on the client company and on you, the client. That's why we want you to spend so much time and effort on recruiting beforehand.

Before you start your search, review the preliminary budget you set up in Chapter 5. It is the price of the ticket that will play an important part in determining the creative resources to whom you will be talking. Why waste time shopping in the wrong places, especially if you do have champagne tastes and beer budgets?

Generally, you can confine your search to six types of businesses: (1) full-service advertising agencies, (2) graphic design firms, (3) audiovisual producers, (4) film/video producers, (5) free-lancers, and (6) marketing communications firms that combine most or all of these disciplines. If you have an in-house agency or design department, you may or may not include it in your search.

Before launching into the steps for selecting these people, let's take a brief look at how they are different.

Full-Service Advertising Agencies

It used to be that full service only meant that the agency could provide the marketing research, create your ads, produce them, and place them in the right media, often leaving graphic design or video services to other resources. Today, agencies are much more multidisciplined and offer much more than in the past—from complete design departments to multimedia services. Marketing research services have become even more customized, with many agencies providing on-line data bases to help their clients with very specifically targeted marketing efforts.

Smaller agencies may offer the same services as larger ones, but they may not do all of them in-house. Whatever the size, for the most part, the people you'll find in any successful agency are highly qualified to work on your project.

Those you will get to know include an *account executive,* an *account coordinator,* and a *writer-art director team.* The account executive (often called "the suit" by agency creatives) is your contact. The account coordinator is someone who will be an account executive in a year or two. He or she is the person you'll call to ask about schedules and the other formalities.

The art director and writer team are just that. Their job is to come up with a creative—and affordable—solution to whatever problem you're trying to solve by producing your project.

You might also get a glimpse of the *creative director*. The writers and art directors report to him or her (or perhaps to a mid-level person called a *creative group head*). The creative director's primary job is to make sure that (a) the marketing problem as you have stated it is properly defined, and (b) that the creative solution reached solves the problem in a way that combines creative flair with solid business judgment.

Typically, you will pay more to have a full-service agency do your work, but you have the advantage of having many services under one roof.

Graphic Design Firms

Most graphic design firms focus solely on the design and production of printed materials that are utilized to support the marketing of a product or service (e.g., packaging, displays, brochures, catalogs, sales sheets, corporate image, and direct mail). Since, by definition, their orientation is graphic rather than textual, the good studios have a stable of crack free-lance copywriters who work contractually, rather than on staff.

The setup of a graphic design firm may be similar to that of an agency: account executive, account coordinator, art director/designer, and lots of computers. Of course, the size of the staff always depends on the size of the firm. Some design firms consist of no more than two graphic designers, two computers, and a dart board. In fact, some of the best work has been known to come out of small studios that started in a garage.

The pricing for work of a similar nature may be just as expensive as the fees charged by a full-service agency. The agencies often offer graphic design services as a convenience to their customers, not as a major profit center. If you are looking to hold the cost down, look at the smaller design firms. They are sometimes just as talented, but because of their lower overhead, they can charge a bit less.

Audiovisual Producers

Most high-end presentations will require the assistance of audiovisual specialists. Although there are computer programs available for doing just about everything yourself, from making slides to creating animation, it is best to bring in the professionals if you want more than "loving hands at home" quality. Good audiovisual producers not only produce your presentation, but also aid you in scripting them and addressing different audiences.

A good audiovisual company can produce anything from single slide shows to multimedia interactive presentations that utilize video, slides, and computer programs. Small companies may simply act as producers, subcontracting all of the pieces. Larger companies have made major investments in equipment and do it all in-house.

Film/Video Producers

Many film/video producers offer the same services as the audio-visual companies. They do, however, specialize in the production of corporate training and sales videos and commercials rather than multimedia presentations.

The level of quality varies tremendously, from the individual who does wedding videos and an occasional corporate job to producers who grew up in the industry and understand the challenges of corporate work.

All audio/visual productions, regardless of size, require the same type of production people. The key players will be the script writer, the producer, the director and the production staff who will do all of the physical work of making the film or tape. Later chapters on video production will describe each of these people and their responsibilities.

Free-lancers

There is a lot of very fine work these days being done by solo practitioners—free-lancers—who choose to operate independently outside the corporate structure.

Some are graphic specialists and designers; others are writers who can pen anything from a brochure to your CEO's speech at the year-end sales meeting. Almost without exception, the free-lance writer has a designer or two with whom he or she works closely, and vice-versa.

The main advantage of hiring free-lancers is that you can usually get the work done more economically—sometimes much more economically—because of low overhead. Very often, free-lancers are refugees from big-time agencies or design firms, so you can find experience and excellence at hurry-and-save prices.

The main disadvantage of working with free-lancers is that they can be a tough sell to your top management. "What do you mean you got this gal who works out of her house and a guy who sits on his boat and writes?!?!" is a fairly common reaction. Another word of caution: sometimes free-lancers cannot handle very large, multifaceted projects or the types of projects that require many bodies.

When looking for free-lancers, make sure to qualify them carefully. Although many are very well qualified, there are also those who took a desktop publishing class or two, bought a computer, hung out a shingle, and know very little about the business.

Some free-lance teams are the best-kept secret in town. They prefer to go solo and limit their projects to what they themselves can handle. But don't be afraid to ask if they can oversee the entire project (or parts of it), just as a larger firm would do. Free-lancers often have contacts that are as good as those of the larger firms, and they can be very helpful as project managers.

Marketing Communications Firms

This is one of those catchall categories that is designed to include anything that hasn't been covered above. These firms can vary from a team of marketing specialists who call on a free-lance network so that they can include creative services in their package to direct mail companies to promotional houses to companies that do nothing more than desktop publishing.

All of them are doing some form of marketing communications, but they are all addressing a different aspect. Some try to offer it all; others only do one small piece. I once met a man who considered himself a marketing communications expert, yet he knew nothing about print advertising or the design and production of sales literature. He sold imported widgets through telemarketing.

The best thing for you to do when you come across these types of professionals is to ask for their brochure, a statement of qualifications, and several references who have used their services for similar work. After nosing around a bit, you should have a firmer grip on who really does what.

Building Your Team

If you're near Detroit or New York or Southern California or Seattle or Portland, creative resources are all around you. But if you are in Tucumcari, New Mexico, or Bath, Maine, you may have to scratch a bit to find the talent you need.

Let's assume you have never before been involved in anything like the new project that was just dumped in your lap. You don't know an advertising agency from the FDIC, so where do you start?

You can start by letting your fingers do the walking. Why not? Every kind of business you'll need is right there in the Yellow Pages, probably even in Tucumcari. But if you live in Orange County, California, and you turn to "Advertising Agencies & Counselors," you'll find about 800 agencies, from the international giants to the lone-wolf outfits.

Unfortunately, all these choices do not make your task easier. You have to cut the squad, so you'll have to start shopping around.

Printers are a good source of information. They work with many different designers and agencies and should be eager to help. After all, at some point somebody will be very anxious to print the end result of your project.

Nevertheless, make sure the printers you contact give you two or three references. Beware of the printer who swears that his pal Louie's Design Delirium is the only game in town.

A few large printers may have an in-house designer or department. You may want to consider working with them, but then that ties you to a single printing source, and all but the very smallest printing jobs should be put out for competitive bid.

Another good bet for referrals will be the advertising manager of your local newspaper, advertising sales representatives for your industry's trade magazines, industry associations, and even your local chamber of commerce. Utilize them for all the same reasons you would a printer, and with all the same caveats.

Nearby universities and community colleges may have curricula in commercial design, advertising and marketing, or both, and the professors in those departments would be worth consulting. Indeed, many of them moonlight in their specialties and may be just the ticket. But be careful if you hire a student to save money. Talent does not mean experience.

Best of all are people in other businesses. Most satisfied customers are pleased to recommend their ad agency or graphics resource—as long as your company is not a competitor. Tradition and professional ethics usually prevent a creative resource from working with more than one client in the same business category.

In sum, there are many different paths to take in getting creative work done, ranging from a full-service advertising agency to lone-wolf free-lancers.

Using the source noted here, you should have no difficulty coming up with a list of candidates. The problem then is to turn that long list into a workable short list.

In our opinion, the best way is to describe the project you have in mind as best you can on a single sheet of paper. Include all the necessary details:

- Type of project
- Number of copies (or desired length, if a video or multimedia)
- Budget
- Deadlines/time frame (preferably expressed in number of weeks or days)

Also note any unusual factors, such as required travel or security precautions (either governmental or competitive), and include a paragraph or two about your company.

Then send this description to the candidates on your long list, with a request to reply by a given date if qualified and interested. Ask them to include a résumé of their business, the clients they serve, the type of work they do best, two current references, and any other information that you, as a prospective client, may find useful. Then sit back and wait.

When the Waiting Is Over

You may end up with anywhere from six to sixty replies. The response will depend in large part on the size of your budget—the more zeros it has, the more potential players will want in the game.

Look over the responses. We will bet that this first screening will enable you to divide the squad into those you feel you might want to work with and those you won't. You will get very strong feelings (one way or the other) about them individually from the way they present themselves.

You will see creativity, quality, and professionalism. Or these qualities will be conspicuous by their absence. This alone should enable you to make your first cut. If there are some fence-sitters, leave them in at this point.

Then call the references they have given, keeping in mind that people rarely offer as a reference someone who will talk in anything but glowing terms. Still, you will get more to add to your "feelings bank."

You should set a goal of arriving at a short list with no more than six candidates. Between the quality of initial presentation (noting carefully how well each has followed your instructions) and the feedback from references, you should be able to make the cut with little difficulty. Again, if you're on the fence with one or two, leave them in; it only means a few more hours of your time.

Then call and ask each short-list candidate to come to your office for a brief capabilities presentation to take no more than forty-five minutes. Some people like to see all the candidates' presentations in one day; others stretch it out for a week or more. There is no rule.

If you are working far enough ahead of your project, we recommend stretching out the interviews. Do one a day, at the same time every day, until you are finished. This gives you the opportunity to think clearly immediately after each presentation and make good notes on each candidate.

You should use an evaluation form (Figure 6.1) so you are consistent in grading each candidate on each criterion. However, you also need to make subjective evaluations, and these will play at least as important a role as the objective criteria.

The problem with interviewing all the short-list candidates in one day is that you seldom have the luxury of time to reflect on your feelings about each candidate—the all-important subjective evaluation.

Of course, you have your own style, and that plays an important role, too. In a very real sense, these sessions are not very different from personnel interviews. If you prefer to interview a dozen job candidates in one day, there's no reason to change now, unless you think stretching it out might be a better way.

Who Says What to Whom?

You listen; the candidates talk. It's their show. Let them soar to the heavens or sink to the depths. But before they take off, do let them know that at some point in the allotted forty-five minutes you will want the answer to a few questions:

- Who are the key people who will actually be working on your project?
- In percentages, what kind of profit does their firm expect to make on your business?
- How important is your business to their shop?
- How much of the creative work they're showing was done by people currently on staff? How much of it was done by the people who will work on your project?
- What positioning and experience do they bring to the project?

If the candidate can't come up with the answers on the spot, that's all right. Tell them that any time in the next twenty-four hours will be fine.

During the presentation period, you'll probably hear a pitch on the firm's background, its clients, and the company's achievements. You'll probably also hear about each firm's business philosophy and its way of working with clients.

Figure 6.1   Evaluation Form

Company: _____

Contact: _____ Phone no. _____

No. of employees: _____ Years in business _____

Rate each of the following on a scale of 1 to 10, with 10 as the highest rating

Work samples

     Creativity   _____

     Neatness   _____

     Originality   _____

     Effectiveness   _____

     Similarity to your needs   _____

     Style   _____

     Versatility   _____

Professionalism

     Organizational skills   _____

     References   _____

     Personal appearance(s)   _____

     Punctuality   _____

     Presentation techniques   _____

     Communication skills   _____

Staff

     Related experience   _____

     Level of comfort with contact   _____

     Management skills   _____

TOTAL   _____

Additional comments: _____

_____

_____

_____

If you hear the presenter talking about the client-agency relationship as a two-way street or a marketing partnership, start paying attention. This signals a good, professional attitude and one that is likely to result in the best work for you.

Then you'll see the ads, the brochures, and the other materials that show off their best work.

Evaluating the Work

What you will see represents, in the firm's opinion, the *very best work* the agency or supplier has *ever* done. Be guided accordingly. If you don't understand the work, ask the presenters to explain it to you.

Does their work all look the same, even though it represents a number of companies in a variety of business categories. Is there a "house style"? If so, you might ask about it. What is their reason for doing everything with a similar "look"? If you don't hear an extremely convincing answer, they are probably not the right folks for you.

If you simply don't like what you see, if it looks amateurish or of poor taste or quality, be inscrutable. Nod your head, smile pleasantly, and respond appropriately. And cross them off your list.

Here are some important questions to answer when reviewing your creative suppliers' samples:

- Is the creative "me too" (that is, does it look like everyone else's work and does every project look alike)?
- Was the work done on budget?
- Were all the deadlines met without trauma? If there was trauma, why did it happen and how was it overcome?
- How many other accounts will be assigned to the account team (or individual) at the same time as yours?
- What percentage of their current business is in the same or a related industry as yours?
- What percentage of their business will your work represent?
- What are some of the case histories (briefly) of the projects they are showing you?

- Were the marketing goals met?
- What effect did the piece or campaign have on sales in actual figures?
- How are typical projects organized?
- Does the agency tell you what type of client they are looking for?
- How is the agency unique?

I was once asked in an interview, "What else would you suggest as a more creative approach to marketing this product (referring to a brochure that the client had on one of his products)?" My first reaction was to reply, "I really would need more information about your project, the market, and the history of what has been done before." Although my client was pleased with my desire to be thorough, he repeated the question, this time adding that he just wanted possibilities, not necessarily the ultimate answer. I then realized he was testing my ability to think quickly and creatively. He was also seeing if I knew how to look at things from a different approach rather than always providing boilerplate answers.

Questions that are a bit out of the norm—such as, "Why did you choose this particular approach?" or "How many ideas did you develop before arriving at this one?"—are excellent for throwing presenters off guard. If they know their stuff, they will be able to respond fairly quickly.

It would be a good idea to write down all the answers. Design a questionnaire based on the examples listed above or create one that will fit your needs.

Beware of the presentation that focuses on the awards the agency has won instead of the results the agency has achieved. I have seen some of the most spectacular, expensive work fail miserably in helping sales. Although awards are a great way for industry peers to applaud each other, few of them are based on results.

I think awards have their place. I've even collected quite a few myself. They do demonstrate the creator's desire to expand his or her thinking as much as possible and to keep everyone sharp in order to compete with others in the industry. However, instead of accepting the awards as the sole demonstration of success, take a closer look at the answers to the questions you asked and the questions they asked.

A lot will be revealed by the answers to your questions. If you find resistance to any of the questions, it may be a hint that the answer is something they do not want you to know. You may discover incompetence, inexperience, unethical or poor business practices, or misrepresentation.

Many years ago a young designer came to my office to show her portfolio. After ten minutes I became suspicious that the work was not all hers. She was too new to the industry to have such an accomplished portfolio. After feeling guilty for presuming the worst, my suspicions were confirmed when she showed me a piece that I had designed and produced. I let her bury herself further by asking her to tell me more about the marketing goals, the budget, and other details of the project. It was amazing how elaborate her story was and, of course, how wrong she was. You should have seen her face when I showed her the art boards that I still had on file.

When analyzing the answers, look to see how clear they were. If the answers didn't make sense or if they skirted the real question, the presenters may not have known the answer. It is easy to be snowed by rhetoric and what is known as "marketing hype."

I once sat in on a sales presentation made by an agency I worked for. They included, as an example of their work, a very elaborate national campaign that included a media buying plan, the creation and production of sales training materials, print ads, television spots, and direct mail. The agency was trying to convince the client of allowing it to do the same thing for the client's product.

In the middle of the presentation, the client's marketing director asked, "Did you know that we have a very limited budget and are only releasing the product on a local level?" I watched the account executive turn pale as he tried to save himself. He had never bothered to find out what the client's goals or plans were. If he had, he could have demonstrated through his examples that he was an effective problem-solver instead of a used car dealer.

It is easy to be dazzled by impressive presentations. Your job is to look past the show and examine the reality. You will need to work with these people very closely. Do they seem to be competent and the type of people that will make your life easier? Look at what happens behind the scenes. If the presentation is just fluff, the questions you asked will help you see how they do business.

Their manner of presentation says a lot about their ability to represent you. Unless the agency specializes in your industry and claims to know everything about it, beware. Do you know everything about the agency's business?

If their thinking seems fuzzy or their ideas seem way off base, they probably aren't right for you. If their presentation or proposal of ideas doesn't flow, most likely that says something about their organizational skills.

Be aware of the "yes man." It is easy to cover incompetence by always agreeing with the client. You want someone who will challenge your ideas and give valid reasons for why the solution may be different from yours. That is what you are paying for; otherwise, you might as well do the job yourself.

On the flip side are the designers, writers, or account executives who are always right. They want to impress you so much with their ability and ideas that they won't listen to any other input.

Take a close look at the presentation. If the presentation does not speak well for the person or company presenting it, how would that translate into the way they would present your company or products? True, the selling approach and objectives may be very different, but you should be able to judge the style, the organization, the creativity, and the results.

Finally, expect to be asked questions about your company, the project, and possibly about future projects. Indeed, you can cross off presenters who do not ask questions. If they aren't doing it in the interview, I would be concerned about their ability to help you with your problem-solving later.

Visiting the Candidates

Now it's time to cut the squad again. Narrow it down to two or three or, at the most, four. Write or call the others and say thanks, but you don't feel they are quite the right match for you.

Then call the survivors and tell them they have made the finals, and you'd like to visit their offices and meet personally with the people who might be working on your project or account. In the case of the lone practitioners, you have already done this, but maybe not with the other half of the team, so you'll want to press on.

In addition to the creatives, you'll also want to talk with the account executive in charge of the business end of your project to determine exactly how the agency wants to work with you financially. If you don't ask some questions about the business end of things up front, you may lose in the end. If the person or agency is in a weak financial position, or if the contract is written poorly, you may ultimately be the one held responsible for the tab, even if you already paid the agency. It may not seem fair, but since you initiated the purchase (e.g., for media space, printing, or model fees), you may end up in court to straighten it out. Whether or not you win, you have lost valuable time and money in a court battle that should never have happened.

Your main goal for the visit should be to see how the creative team operates on its own turf. It may be very different from the formal presentation you heard in your office.

In addition to your initial visit, you may want to stop by for a second visit. Just wait a few days, call, and ask for the account executive or your contact person. If neither one is available, ask for someone else who may be on the creative team or someone who knows the company well, such as an administrator. Explain that you just wanted a chance to stop by again and talk to some people and take a closer look at the operation.

The agency people may either scurry around in a panic or invite you in with a smile and help you in any way they can. Especially in the larger agencies, the staff may not even know who you are. Often members of the creative team aren't aware of potential clients until there is a real chance that they may get the account and it's time to become involved in the creative presentation.

During your second visit, you may have more time to speak to some of the staff that you had not previously met. In rare instances, you may notice that some faces are missing, and when you ask where they are, your tour guide may stutter and stammer about their whereabouts.

Years ago, when I was a free-lancer for ad agencies, I was called in more than once to act as "fill" in order to make it seem as though there were more full-time staff members than actually existed. The potential client would come through, and then I would leave. It was an old trick that worked well to fill otherwise empty desks and to make the shop look even busier. Don't expect deception; it's far from the norm. Simply be aware that seeing is not always believing and that some agencies may resort to questionable tactics when trying to impress a potential client.

Your second visit will also give you the chance to see the everyday work environment, instead of the cleaned-up version. This is not to say that there is always a difference between the two. Most agencies and design studios try to maintain a professional setting. However, it is good to see people in action when they are not prepared for a visitor.

Making Your Decision

By now, you've put what seems like a tremendous amount of work into this project and you haven't even started yet! Well, you have, actually. You've tossed out two of the final six candidates, but what now?

If you're a normal person, you have some very mixed emotions by now. You like this outfit's creative samples the best, but you liked that outfit's people the best. Alice's fees were higher than Joe's, but you liked her range of experience in the industry. On the other hand, you felt that working with Joe would be easier.

And so it goes. Conflict. One way out is to contrast the pros and cons of each finalist. An adapted evaluation form can help you rate the finalists in each category and total the scores based on your evaluations. (See Figure 6.2.)

You may find that even after you do that there are still three candidates tied for first. That's progress. At least one has been eliminated. Now you need to review all the facts and feelings about the three who remain.

Wait a day or two, then compare the finalists again. Maybe this time a clear winner will emerge—and maybe not. However, you'll almost always be able to whittle the list down to two.

Figure 6.2   Finalist Comparisons

A. Name: _____   Phone: _____

B. Name: _____   Phone: _____

C. Name: _____   Phone: _____

Rate each of the following on a scale of 1 to 10, with 10 as the highest rating.

	A	B	C
Work samples			
Creativity	___	___	___
Neatness	___	___	___
Originality	___	___	___
Effectiveness	___	___	___
Similarity to your needs	___	___	___
Style	___	___	___
Versatility	___	___	___
Professionalism			
Organizational skills	___	___	___
References	___	___	___
Personal appearance(s)	___	___	___
Punctuality	___	___	___
Presentation techniques	___	___	___
Communication skills	___	___	___
Staff			
Related experience	___	___	___
Level of comfort with contact	___	___	___
Management skills	___	___	___
TOTAL	___	___	___

Then, if all else fails, go with your gut feeling. Go with the chemistry. Go with the people you feel you will be able to work with better, from whom you may coax some extra effort.

Whether your choice is a solo practitioner, a full-service agency, or something in between, now that you've put this much effort into the process of selecting the right creative resources for you and your company, you really can't go wrong.

Now you have to learn to work with them.

CHAPTER 7

Working with Your Creative Resources

You are now what's known in the trades as *the client.* This term is not unlike the Hawaiian word *aloha,* which can mean hello, goodbye or many other things. How you begin the interaction with your resources tells them up front what they can expect from you and what you expect from them. It is really up to you to set the stage for your involvement in the project and to establish the type of client you will be (a prepared and knowledgeable one!).

In your erg list you established who will do what, when, where and how. You have also prepared a preliminary budget. Now you are ready to form an agreement with your suppliers and give them the green light to begin work.

But what if you aren't ready to set everything in stone because you aren't sure what the creative folks will recommend? How can you enter an agreement when you aren't sure yet what it will include? This can be a frustrating situation, but the dilemma isn't as bad as it appears.

Small Steps: The Estimate and Contingencies

In most projects, nobody can tell you how much something is going to cost until some ideas are on paper. If the project is not yet clearly defined, the first financial commitment you may make will be a *development fee*—a professional charge very much like an attorney's retainer. As with a retainer, it is often paid up front.

The development fee enables your creative resource to spend time meeting with you, getting your input, and, from that contact, to spend more time arriving at preliminary creative solutions to your project.

Such rough solutions enable your creatives to make better estimates of how much each of the ideas will cost to produce. At this point they should be nothing more than fairly reliable ballpark estimates.

From there on, it gets easy. You pick one of the solutions for development, your creatives develop it and they come back to you with pretty layouts and the final *production cost estimate* (PCE), which is complete down to sales tax and delivery and should include the information in Figure 5.2.

When it is time to draw up an agreement based on these costs, it may contain language to the effect that: "Client is liable for payment only to the extent of approved charges contained in the production cost estimate and subsequent revisions of same, if any."

Of course, realistically, there will be revisions. You'll decide to change things, the unexpected will happen, your CEO won't like his suit in his photo, whatever. The creative resource may come to you and say, "Hey, boss, we kind of blew this retouching estimate and we'll need an *extra $700,000.*" You're a firm believer that nobody should be penalized for a little mistake like that, so you sign off on the *revised* PCE. (Not really, but you get the idea.)

Any creative resource with half a brain will include in its PCE a *contingency* figure of anywhere from 10 to 20 percent. This is included to cover executive mind-changes, rainy days, unexpected retouching of hair transplants, and a variety of human errors.

Contingencies are good, not bad, because the alternative is for your creative resource to pad here and there until the PCE is a work of fiction. Since creating and producing the tools of marketing is mostly art and very little science, honest mistakes will be made. Certain seemingly simple events—photography sessions, usually—will turn nightmarish, other pieces of work will have to be redone because they just didn't turn out as well as everybody thought they would. Those and many other reasons are why contingencies were invented.

The whole point of these precautions is to ensure that when your project is completed and bills are in, there are no surprises lurking in the lower right corners of your invoices.

Faithful changing of estimates as the job evolves and a willingness to accept the contingency system will keep the surprises away and help preserve a good business relationship between you and your creative resource.

The Service Contract (Figure 7.1)

This is a must. No project, regardless of size, should be started without one. Everyone involved needs to understand exactly what is expected of everyone else. The whole idea is to head off any of those dreadful finger-pointing arguments that stem from misunderstandings.

Curiously, service agreements are often more necessary in short-term special-project relationships than they are in the ongoing alliances most advertisers and their agencies have. In an ongoing alliance, once several projects are completed, both sides know how things are done. They have developed a level of trust based on experience. (If they haven't, it's time to re-evaluate the relationship!)

On the other hand, short-term relationships or special projects are often done with new suppliers. Or, sometimes the supplier and client contact have worked together, but one of them is with a new company. In either case, the situation is new and requires even more attention to detail.

The bottom line is that what needs to exist is some form of agreement—or two agreements—that covers the interests of you, the client and the service provider you are retaining. When you finally make the agreement, do it in writing and have all parties sign it. You and your supplier can decide just how complex it needs to be. But, remember, a nod of the head and a handshake may reinforce your trust in each other, but they don't serve to clarify details that can be misunderstood.

Miscellaneous Possibilities and the Unexpected

Although most agreements tend to cover the same type of information, there are always those fine points that seem to fall between the cracks. You know, the ones that your last vendor never worried about. The ones that get you while you aren't looking.

I hate surprises. You probably feel the same. But I have seen more than one potential client freak at the details in my agreements. I always explain that it is not a trust issue but one of common sense. It's all there, in black and white. No surprises. It really is better that way and tends to build a stronger relationship. I have nothing to hide and I hope my clients don't either.

Take a glance at Figure 7.1. In addition to the usual scope of work and payment schedule descriptions, there are points on termination, ownership, press proofs, expenses and additional charges. Let's take a look at the various parts of the agreement.

Establishing Deadlines

Most projects usually point to some event. An annual report must be published by the stockholders' meeting. The brochure and video for your company's revolutionary new glanchometer have to be ready for the winter trade show. You are dust if the slide presentation isn't ready for the annual sales meeting.

So certainly your side of the agreement has to cover a commitment to deliver by the date you specify. But what happens if your creative resources don't deliver as promised? What happens if the printer has a press breakdown or strike?

The best answer is to not get yourself into that kind of jam in the first place. We talked about that in the chapter on setting a schedule. But now we're talking about how to cover the countless possible things that can go wrong in a simple service agreement.

Basically, there isn't much you can do about it, save calling in the lawyers. The good news is, most projects somehow get done on time regardless of how many things went wrong and regardless of whose fault it was. But if you want to protect yourself, include a reduced payment if the deadline is not met. Of course, what good is a discount when the trade show will go on with or without your printed materials.

You need to uphold your end of the bargain if your suppliers must meet theirs. They can't be expected to adhere to a contract deadline if you don't provide what they need to meet the schedule.

Figure 7.1   Sample Service Contract

Date: _____

Client: _____

Client Address: _____

Client Phone #: _____

Project: _____

From (designer or agency contact): _____

Estimated Total Cost: (see attached estimate) $ _____

Terms: _____% of all art charges will be invoiced upon approval of estimate. Remainder of all art charges to be invoiced upon delivery of final artwork. _____% of film and printing to be billed upon release of artwork to printer. Balance of film and printing to be billed upon delivery of printed materials. If the project is not completed within two weeks of the date of initial invoice, all outstanding charges will be billed at that time. In adherence to trade customs and procedures, liability for any errors, except those of a technical nature related to the printing process, rests with the client once approvals for finished artwork have been signed off by the client.

Payment Schedule: All payments are due _____ days from date of invoice.

Termination: If work is terminated by either party before completion of this project, all fees plus supplier expenses will be billable up to the point of termination. Losses caused by the termination of thie contract (such as liabilities for reserved advertising space or scheduling of suppliers), shall be paid by the client.

Ownership: the client has the following rights to the artwork and copywriting created in this project: _____

_____

_____

All rights not expressly granted in this agreement remain the exclusive property of the designer (or copywriter or agency). Artwork created for use in this project by the vendors (i.e., illustrators, photographers) of the designer/agency is the property of those vendors and may not be used without permission. The approved usage beyond the scope of this project will be billed at prevailing rates unless otherwise predetermined. Full rights and usage will be determined and agreed upon in writing. Client shall return all artwork within 60 days from completion of project.

Press proofs: Unless the client is present when the plate is made ready for the press, so that no press time is lost, presses standing waiting the approval of the customer will be charged at current rates for the time consumed. If the client chooses not to be at the press check, XYZ Agency will not be held responsible for the approval of the press sheet.

Figure 7.1 Sample Service Contract *(continued)*

Overruns and Underruns: Due to the nature of printing, up to a 10% variance of quantity may occur. The client will be billed according to the exact quantity that is delivered.

Additional Charges: This agreement is based on the project and services described in the attached estimate. It does not include charges for revisions due to changes requested by the client in the scope or design of the project as described; if such changes are necessary, they will be estimated in advance and billed separately, and the client agrees to pay such charges. Suppliers' charges are approximate pending final approval of layout and copy. The client will be notified, in writing, of any changes in these portions of the estimate.

Expenses: Mileage, long-distance telephone calls, photocopies, postage, messenger services, and cartage are not included and will be billed in addition to the charges above. These charges will not exceed $100 without prior client approval. Travel charges (airfare, hotel, etc.) related to the job will be billed additionally.

Scheduling: The designer/agency is not responsible for meeting the production schedule should the client fail to provide the required materials to complete the project based on that schedule.

Production Schedule: The production schedule is due as follows: concept and initial layouts _____, final layouts _____, final copy _____, production art _____, printing _____, other (describe) _____.

Note: If work does not begin on this project within 30 days, we are permitted to submit revised estimates reflecting any cost changes. If work begun is subsequently delayed, or placed on hold, the project will be re-estimated to reflect prevailing costs before continuing.

Please indicate your approval by signing and returning one copy. Your signature gives _____ the authority to undertake the work described in this estimate and to bill in accordance with the terms stated. Your signature also indicates your acceptance of all costs, terms, and provisions of this estimate. In the event that litigation occurs due to any aspect of the project, the losing party agrees to pay all court and attorney fees.

Duly signed by an authorized agent.

Name:_____ Date: _____

Company: _____ Title: _____

Name:_*Joe Schwartz*_____ Date: *00/00/00*_____

Company: *XYZ Agency*_____ Title: *Senior Account Executive*_____

The best way to make sure of this is to advise your boss in advance of the time schedule and of the company's time frame. If there are changes, so advise all parties. And do all of it in writing.

The following kind of wording to allow for revised schedules and to ensure that all parties are satisfied has proven successful: "Project work shall be performed according to the production schedule, and its revisions, approved by both parties."

The Dollar Dilemma

There are two basic kinds of budget problems: (1) the client feels he or she is overcharged; (2) the creative source feels he or she is being paid too slowly. Obviously, there can be a serious problem here— possibly a deal breaker—but it can be fixed or avoided altogether.

You do it in the agreement. One part says that Demonic Design will provide the client with cost estimates for each phase of the job. The client will sign off on those estimates and will not pay for work that has not been approved. Simple. Another part states that you agree to pay your vendor's invoices within a specified time period. That is why terms are defined clearly in the agreement. If the agreement isn't complete, some-body may end up getting hurt. And it shouldn't be you.

Let me share a story that was told to me by one of my students. The first night of class I would always ask why the students chose to take my class. One young woman sheepishly raised her hand. She then shared her incredible story.

"My boss told me I had to take your class before working with any more graphic designers."

"Why is that?" I asked.

"Well, I hired a designer to do our corporate brochure. I told her the budget was $35,000 to design it. About a couple of weeks later she returned with some incredible ideas, things I never would have thought of doing."

"So why was that a problem?" I responded.

"The problem was that our final bill was $108,000."

I couldn't imagine what this brochure looked like with that kind of a price tag. This would be a very expensive corporate brochure for

Figure 7.2   Sample Agency Retainer Agreement

Date _____

(Agency name) _____ will provide advertising, marketing, graphic design, public relations, consultation and account management of promotions for (company name) _____.

This agreement formalizes the scope of services (agency name) _____ will provide and the general terms and conditions under which these services will be performed.

First, this agreement acknowledges (agency name) _____ as the exclusive advertising agency and agency of record for (company name) _____, responsible for all advertising and public relations functions.

This agreement also authorizes (agency name) _____ to make any and all mutually agreed upon commitments for materials, services, and media placement in your name and on your behalf.

In return for performing these mutually agreed upon services, the agency will be compensated according to the following schedule:

Account Service/Retainer

Initially, the agency will receive a retainer of $_____ per month for performing the following service functions:

Account Management
Account Coordination
Marketing Consultation
Weekly Meetings
Budget Planning
Advertising and Promotion Strategy
Creative Concepts and Art Direction

This monthly retainer is due and payable in advance on the first of every month

Creative/Public Relations/Marketing Services

Additional advertising, marketing, and public relations services and special projects will be handled on a job-by-job basis as agreed upon by (company name) _____ and (agency name) _____.

(continued)

Figure 7.2 Sample Agency Retainer Agreement *(continued)*

All prices will be agreed upon in writing prior to job commencement. All agency buyouts (such as photography, art, design, illustration, printing, or services of vendors related to promotional activities) will be billed in addition to the retainer fee.

Media

Media placement, development of media plans and schedules to meet your needs and budgetary perameters, contract negotions with media, media billing coordination, and tearsheets will be handled by the Agency. Agency will purchase the lowest possible advertising rate for the Client's account and will receive 15% commission directly from the Client as compensation for media services where applicable. Client will be directly responsible for all media bills.

Expenses

Out-of-pocket expenses incurred by the Agency on the Client's account for shipping, delivery, long-distance telephone calls, and travel beyond sixty (60) miles will be billed to the Client at the Agency's cost, without commission or markup.

Certain jobs of inordinate expense may require 50% of the job's costs to initiate work. In such events, the balance of the Client's payment will be due and payable within thirty (30) days, unless otherwise stipulated in the mutually agreed upon written job production agreement.

Terms

All agency billing will be issued as follows: 1/3 of estimated costs upon initiation of project, 1/3 of estimated costs upon completion of artwork production, and balance of final charges upon completion of project. Invoices are payable upon receipt, due within thirty (30) days of invoice date, with one and one-half percent (1-1/2%) due on all billings over thirty (30) days.

In adherence to trade customs and procedures, liability for any errors, except those of a technical nature related to the printing process, rests with the Client once approvals for finished artwork have been signed off by the Client.

Note: If work does not begin on projects within thirty (30) days, we are permitted to submit revised estimates reflecting any cost changes. If work begun is subsequently delayed, or placed on hold, the projects will be re-estimated to reflect prevailing costs before continuing. Estimates are approximate and are

Figure 7.2   Sample Agency Retainer Agreement *(continued)*

based on the project and services described. They do not include charges for revisions due to changes requested by the Client in the scope or design of the project as described; if such changes are necessary, they will be estimated in advance and billed separately, and the Client agrees to pay such charges. Suppliers' charges are approximate pending final approval of layout and copy. Client will be notified of any changes in these portions of the estimates.

Indemnification

In performing its services for the Client, the Agency may rely on the accuracy and lawfulness of all information and material furnished by the Client to the Agency concerning the Client's products and services. The Client shall indemnify and hold the Agency harmless from and against all costs, expenses, and liabilities incurred in or in connection with any such claim or proceeding brought thereon. Agency shall not be liable to the Client or to any other person whatsoever for any damage occasioned by the failure of performance or unsatisfactory performance on the part of any medium or vendor.

The parties agree and understand that if any action is necessary to enforce the terms of this agreement, the prevailing party is entitled to reasonable attorney's fees and costs, in addition to any other relief to which the party may be entitled.

Period of Contract

This agreement will remain in force through _____, commencing _____. It may be terminated at any time by either party by giving the other party not less than ninety (90) days prior notice in writing, sent to the principal place of business of the Agency or Client.

Agreed and Accepted:

Company name: _____

By: _____

Title: _____

Date: _____

Company name: _____

By: _____

Title: _____

Date: _____

a small company, or for *any* company. So I asked, "Would you like to share with us how that happened?"

"The brochure ended up being twice as many pages as we asked for. The designer also added a pocket folder and inserts. Then, upon her suggestion, we sent a photographer and his assistant to all kinds of places out of state to get some distinctive shots. That was all very expensive. Especially because our President didn't like most of them, so we had to reshoot. Finally, the printing ended up being 7 color because of some special inks she wanted to use. It just seemed to keep adding up."

Then I asked the one question that this poor woman had failed to ask her designer, "Didn't you ask up front what the fees would include, before committing to all of that?"

Her reply sent a chill up my spine, "Well, sort of. When I told her we had a $35,000 budget to 'design' a brochure, that is exactly what she charged. I just didn't realize that 'design' did not include the production, art, photography, revisions, art direction, copywriting or printing. I guess I was a real fool."

Hopefully, most creative suppliers will be clear and up front about what their fees include. If you ever run across one that isn't, insist that they spell it out on paper. Review it, discuss it if you are unclear of what it all means, then sign it.

Whose Artwork Is This?

My experience is that the most discussed point in the agreement is who owns what. Later on in the book I will discuss *ownership* versus *usage*. For the sake of discussion right now, all you need to know is that you should never assume you own it just because you paid for it.

There are very clear laws about usage rights. They apply to photography, illustration, artwork, and copywriting. There are also laws of ownership about film and printing plates. Some suppliers are more flexible than others. Don't find out the hard way whether or not your suppliers are sticklers about ownership. It can be a very costly mistake.

Don't think you can skirt around this one. That guy Murphy loves to apply his law here. Some time ago I used stock photography for a client's brochure. I purchased the rights to use the photos in an ad campaign and a brochure. That was all.

I made sure my client understood the limitations on the usage, and fortunately I got this in writing. The client purchased his own printing and borrowed the photos for a short time so that they could be used by the printer.

Two weeks later, I showed up at the trade show. To my surprise, I found huge blow-ups of every photo displayed at the booth. I warned my client that he had not purchased the rights to use the photos in this way. He assured me I was being ridiculous to worry.

Guess what! I received a big bill from the stock photo house for the additional usage. My client refused to pay. I had my written agreement signed by the client, stating the limitations. He still refused to pay. In fact, he had already had duplicates made of the photos so that he could use them for other things.

After threats of lawsuits by my supplier and myself and lots of name-calling (under my breath, of course), the client paid, six months later. I'll never know how the supplier knew that my client used the photos for more than the original agreement. I do know that I have repeated this story many times when clients question the chance of being caught.

CHAPTER 8

Creating an In-House Department:
Pros and Cons

Before computers changed the way we do business, the decision of whether or not to set up an in-house art department was not difficult. If a company generated enough work to support one or more artists full time, it made sense to buy a drawing board, some markers and pens, a T square, glue, and other supplies and create an in-house art department.

Today the decision is more complex. Technology-based equipment (e.g., computers, scanners, modems, printers, and software) is a major investment. Furthermore, the training and knowledge required to operate these machines require more than a simple understanding of good design principles and how to paste up camera-ready copy.

Although the computer has revolutionized the industry, it has also been the source of a lot of frustration and lost revenue. So if you have any thoughts of doing your creative work in-house, read this chapter very carefully.

The In-House Art Department

There are many kinds and sizes of in-house art departments. Some consist of one computer and one designer (or—perish the thought—a computer with no designer, but a couple of people who took a course in desktop publishing). Others may consist of a marketing communications director and one or more graphic designers. Some are so elaborate that they have a full creative staff (including writers) and possibly even their own printing press. It is not uncommon for larger companies to set up their own in-house advertising agency that operates autonomously from the rest of the company, yet meets all the advertising and marketing communications needs of the parent company.

The size and type of in-house art department is usually based on the level of volume and quality required by the company. For example, most major retailers have very large staffs to produce their daily ads or mailers. Companies that are printing-intensive because of their frequent use of direct mail sometimes find it more economical to buy their own printing company.

Of course, there are many pros and cons to consider when deciding if it is (a) worthwhile to set up an in-house department and (b) economical to use the department. The decision usually comes down to money and time!

Let's start by making the assumption that your company is seeing a steadily increasing volume of marketing materials purchased from outside vendors. It has become apparent that the investment in personnel and equipment would be worthwhile investigating. Now, without trying to burst your bubble of excitement, let me offer a checklist of questions you should answer before making your decision.

Checklist 6. Evaluating Your Needs for In-House Creative Services

☐ How much does your company spend annually on marketing communications materials?

☐ How much of the production of your materials would you propose to do in-house (e.g., writing, artwork, photography)?

☐ What are you currently spending on the services you plan to bring in-house?

☐ How much will it cost for equipment, salaries, benefits, and other overhead costs (such as rent, utilities, and supplies) for those employees?

☐ Will your current space allow for the addition of new employees?

☐ Can anyone on your current staff adequately supervise the new department with thorough knowledge and understanding of how an art department functions?

☐ Will the supervisor have adequate time to run this new department?

☐ Will the final cost of running the department (amortize the initial start-up costs over a three- or five-year period) be more or less than your projected costs of using outside vendors over the next three to five years?

☐ Will this department place an administrative strain on your current staff?

☐ Will an in-house art department provide enough versatility and creativity for your projects?

If nobody on your staff has the experience to make these evaluations, you may consider bringing in a marketing communications consultant to assist you. In fact, you may also consider hiring this type of person as a staff member once you make the commitment to create an in-house art department.

Remember, the creative business is not the same as yours. Don't let a little bit of knowledge get in your way. Rely on an experienced professional to guide you. In the long run, it may be more economical and less taxing than steering existing personnel into uncharted waters.

There are also many consultants available to assist you in selecting, purchasing, and installing the correct equipment. They can be very helpful, but be cautious because they can also be glorified salespeople with more on their agenda than setting up a cost-effective system.

Weighing the Pros and Cons

So, you did your homework and you still think an in-house art department is a great idea. You're ready to start writing the checks to make it happen.

Not so fast. The "in-house" concept *is* great. But, frankly it isn't for everyone. Before you jump in gleefully with both feet, take a look again at the entire picture. You may have missed some of the following bits of wisdom (provided by those who speak from experience).

Why You Should Create an In-House Department

- The markups added by agencies or designers are eliminated.
- Media dollars are saved by buying directly.
- The education process is shorter because employees are more aware of the product and company developments.
- The company has more control over the work, making it easier to
  ◇ Get work done faster
  ◇ Meet deadlines more efficiently
  ◇ Do revisions
  ◇ Review work in progress
  ◇ Provide daily input
- Greater consistency is achieved because the designer is involved in the daily process of the company.
- The tendency for unnecessary "fluff" is lessened.
- If the project doesn't go full cycle, no money is wasted on outside services that have already started to fulfill their contracts.
- You know exactly what to expect because you always know with whom you are working.
- "Task" teams (e.g., marketing, sales, engineering, and design) can meet more quickly and don't have to wait for appointments with outside services.
- The in-house team is more entrenched in daily routines, making it easier to understand the needs of the company and the ways to accommodate management to make a project work.
- You are more in touch with how far you can go on a project without bypassing the boundaries.

- It is easier to meet the parameters of existing criteria.
- You can still use outside vendors when necessary.

Why You Shouldn't Create an In-House Department

- An outside agency may be able to see with a clearer focus what is going on in the industry.
- The outside agency may have better access to and knowledge of resources.
- You may not be able to afford to cover all the areas of expertise you need in order to do the job right (e.g., software, hardware, people).
- Many in-house heads are creators, not organizers, which leads to organizational problems.
- Additional personnel means more personnel hurdles.
- Management may not understand what is needed to make things happen, resulting in unrealistic expectations.
- Larger departments have more equipment; therefore, there is more equipment that can break down.
- The rest of your company may be in a different operating environment on the computer, therefore causing a compatibility problem with the typical environment used by designers.
- The creative team may end up working in a vacuum, especially if the department is very small.
- Sometimes the marketing communications manager can't do the job to the level you would like because he or she is juggling too many administrative responsibilities while managing the creative work.
- The head of the in-house department may not be trained for that responsibility. If not, he or she won't have a real understanding of the production process. This can lead to *very* expensive problems.
- There is more flexibility when working with outside vendors.

- The in-house department does not usually promote a creative mentality.
- It is difficult to convert existing personnel into creative resources.

The Equipment Crazies

Unless you have very deep pockets, the initial expense of setting up your department may seem exorbitant. Of course, there is also the frustration of knowing that whatever equipment you buy, within six months, something faster, better, and less expensive will be introduced.

Don't be dismayed. Everyone around you is in the same boat. Just do what you can do. Don't be afraid to ask a lot of questions. Call service bureaus (listed in the Yellow Pages under "pre-press") and ask for their recommendations. Ask other companies what they purchased. Talk to some designers. Attend seminars and classes. And read, then read, and read some more. There are several good publications that review products and list several mail order companies for price comparisons.

Depending on how big you want to start, there are a wide range of options for equipment available. If you are starting small, make sure you buy something that can be expanded later. Some of the less expensive equipment is great for starters, but may not meet your needs down the line. Look forward one year to 18 months because the equipment and your needs change rapidly.

Don't forget to ask about software. Usually the hardware decisions are based on what software you plan to use.

If you are only bringing in a staff writer, a simple PC with a word processing program may be adequate. On the other hand, designers require computers with a capability to operate the types of programs needed to create artwork. And that artwork has to be generated in a format compatible with the printers who make the film and the printing plates. So, the equipment has to be right, or you will pay at the other end.

As a last word about equipment: Make sure you really understand what you are buying. Know about the equipment, its function, capability, limitations, service and most of all, compatibility.

If you still feel totally overwhelmed by the confusion of the technology, a word of encouragement: You can do it! If an entire industry based on right-brained people (the ad biz) can do it, so can you. Besides, you can always set up your department without a computer and stick to the tried and true method of using board, paper and glue.

When all else fails, go back to your outside vendors. I'm sure they'd love to see you again.

CHAPTER 9

Making the Project Go

You did it. You selected a team that will knock the socks off even the toughest boss. The products are ready. Nobody in charge of approvals is leaving town for awhile. You have finally taken care of all the paperwork. You even bought one of those scheduling boards to show how well you are keeping on track.

If you followed the steps in this book to this point, you should be able to trust the creative resources with whom you will be working.

Your definition of the project and its objectives should be *very* clear by now. You know what the assignment is, and you have communicated it precisely to the members of your creative team.

Let's face it, the expression "garbage in, garbage out" doesn't apply only to the computer business. If you don't have a handle on the project, no one else will either—and you just may get what's coming to you!

Now what? Although your role has in no way diminished, it is your turn to kick back a little and let your creative team go to work. It's time to wait patiently while the cogs of creativity are churning. Meanwhile, continue doing what you always do, whether it's managing other projects or running a school.

Before you know it, the creative team members will be back with their initial concepts.

Understanding Creatives

Because of the nature of their talents and work, the members of your creative team are probably a little different from you. They probably think differently and may even dress quite differently. But if you've been as thorough in the screening process as we have recommended, you will be working with people who are just as businesslike as you are. They sometimes have an unusual way of showing it.

Good creatives are experts at communicating with people on an emotional level. To be successful, they often employ unusual methods of getting the job done.

If you were able to witness your creative team in action (a word of caution: don't do it unless you're invited; this is just a hypothetical situation to help you understand the process), you may see individuals throwing darts, sitting on the floor with paper everywhere, or even listening to music under a tree in the park.

I can't tell you how many times friends or clients have asked, "How did you come up with that idea?" I honestly can't tell them, but I did— and it worked.

The thing to remember is that the salespeople, engineers, accountants, computer experts,, doctors, carpenters, clerks, buyers, rocket scientists—whatever audience you need to reach—are all human beings too. They respond to a variety of stimuli. They have a sense of humor. They have hot buttons that can be pressed and heart strings that can be plucked. The creative people are trained to reach all these people, whatever their methods of arriving at the right approach.

This is precisely why you are not creating the project. You are not a writer nor a designer nor a video director. You have hired people who are as professional in their jobs as you are in yours—even if their best ideas come while they're throwing darts. Now you must let them flourish.

Give them direction, objectives, and all the information they can absorb and more. Then stand back and let them do what you're paying them to do.

What to Expect

The first thing your creative team might do is disagree with you. Good creatives are not supposed to think the way you do. They're supposed to think the way your customers do. Thus, after receiving your input, they may go to their corners and come up with some new wrinkles on the definition of your problem or, indeed, an entirely new definition.

In fact, if the creatives don't challenge you a little, you should start worrying about whether you've hired the right people.

Cliché no. 173 among creatives says that it is not their job to give you what they think you want or what you may be expecting. It is the job of top professionals to give you what you need. And that is why they must have the best input you can give them—all the details, all the research, all the objectives.

This fact applies at all levels whether you only need a sales sheet or a full-blown ad campaign. How effective will it be if it isn't right?

So be willing to listen to new ideas or unusual solutions. Don't fall back on the traditional or the mediocre. Don't be afraid of a good idea, however unique. Approach the proposed solutions with an open mind.

The Search for Ideas

Once everyone involved has agreed on where the project is supposed to go, it is the creative team's job to figure out how to get there. While you are catching up on your other work, they will be shaping and molding shreds of ideas into one that will work for you. This stage is called *concepting.*

During this stage the art person and the word person will most likely argue about what works and what doesn't. While there does come a time when the designer designs and the copywriter writes, at this point there is no division of labor.

Unless, of course, their task is totally exclusive of the other. Like when you provide the artist with copy. Or perhaps you just need copy because you will do the art in-house.

The wordsmith will often come up with a visual idea and the artist will just as often coin a zingy phrase or a headline that says it all! All that matters is how good the ideas are and whether or not they solve the problem. A good creative team might end up with a dozen or more ideas and themes stuck on their wall, or they may only have two or three that do the same job.

The next step is the internal critical review. The specifics of this process depend on the type and size of organization. In a large or highly structural organization the next step might be a revision of surviving concepts by the supervisors. In a small, independent firm or with individual free-lancers, the next step might be a cooling-off period before the concepts are revised and evaluated.

The *thumbnails* (the chicken scratches representing the ideas) are pawed over and insulted, critiqued and criticized, discussed and evaluated. The overriding question is whether the ideas solve the marketing problem as defined and agreed upon. Beyond that, do they project the image the client needs? And, of major importance, can they be produced on time and on budget, or as closely as possible? Beware of creative resources who have a "dynamite idea" that will only run a few thousand dollars over budget.

The Presentation of Ideas

After you've stuffed your creatives with the appropriate information and turned them loose, a team will be ready to take you on a journey through idealand. Invite a few knowledgeable passengers to accompany you on this trip.

During this presentation, devote your full attention to what you are seeing. Don't take any phone calls; don't sign any memos; don't, if possible, get up to go to the bathroom.

Bear in mind that at this stage you are looking for a brilliant idea, not the masterful execution of the idea. Please listen carefully as each concept is presented to you and give each idea a fair hearing. Let the creatives explain their thought process and tell you why and how the ideas solve the problem as defined.

The form of the creative team's presentation depends on you. How well can you visualize? Does anybody else have to see the work at this point? If the answers, in order, are "Very well" and "No," then you can save money and time by attending the presentation alone. You will be examining what are called *roughs, tissues, organizationals,* or *loose comps (comprehensives)*—the terms vary greatly.

Regardless of terminology, what you'll see is a roughly sketched presentation of ideas, sometimes at full size, often at half or quarter scale. At this point, your creative team is trying to communicate ideas. Nobody is concerned with the details of executing the ideas.

Finding the Winning Idea

It only takes one idea to make a winner, but finding that idea is like drilling for oil. You sometimes have to sink a lot of holes before striking the one that makes you rich. Likewise, creatives often have to go down dead-end streets as well as fast-paced superhighways before finding the right idea for you.

This, however, brings up the controversial point of how many ideas should be presented. Frankly, the amount of creative development money that you have given your resource will determine the amount of thinking that will go into your project. Logically, the more thinking, the better the ideas.

Some creatives, especially when dealing with relatively low-budget projects, will show the client only one or two ideas. Of course, sometimes it does happen that after hours of thinking, the first idea is still the best. But good creatives do not want to overlook other possibilities.

Sometimes it is worthwhile for the creative team to present three or four rough ideas and maybe a large pile of hen scratches that represent other forays in search of a solution. It really depends on the project and the client.

Some clients don't want to be bothered with an elaborate, thorough presentation. They just want to see a few possibilities, and they want to feel confident that the ideas are on target.

I believe that clients deserve to know how recommendations were reached. That sometimes means showing some of the rejects. There are always many creative solutions to any given problem, and the folks who are paying the bill deserve to know what is going on.

On the other hand, while I believe in giving clients a choice, I do not present any ideas that I do not feel comfortable recommending. I've seen others do it, and it was not a pretty sight. The designers had a couple of good ideas, but they wanted to flesh out the presentation. So they brought in an idea from the cast-off pile—and, you guessed it—that's the one the client picked.

A Few Words of Advice

Even if you see one idea that is so good you want to cry, hold off. Live with all the ideas for a few days. Roll them around in your head, especially if the end product is something your company will be living with for a long time.

At this stage, don't fall into the opinion trap. Showing the rough layouts to everyone from the director to the office clerk and asking for opinions needlessly complicates the decision-making process. No one else knows the project as well as you, and no one else can provide an informed evaluation. The decision is yours to make.

However, if you are still not comfortable with any of the ideas, have another session with your creatives. They may have had the right idea but the wrong way of selling it. Call them back and see how passionate they are about how good and how right the ideas are for your company. Then rethink your decision.

If your instincts are right and the work is all wrong, you have two choices. You either send your team back to the drawing board or you pick a new team. If you are confident that you chose the right people in the first place, then stick with them.

Whatever your decision, be specific. Tell your creative team precisely why you think that what it has done doesn't work and how it might be remedied. No one can improve an idea based on the old cop-out, "It just doesn't move me."

Let's say that everybody got lucky on this one. You saw three different concepts, and the biggest problem you had with them is figuring out which one was the greatest. Actually, that happens more often than not. There are far more happy tales than horror stories.

We had a client once for whom we did one project a month for more than fifteen years, and we only had to go back to the drawing board three or four times. The reasons are quite simple. We usually had plenty of time to think, we always offered at least two solutions, and the client gave us plenty of information and guidance. And without exception, we gave him what he needed, not necessarily what he was expecting. Chances are you'll be in this situation too. Then all you have to do is kick the project along and make it go.

To Comp or Not to Comp

Once you have reviewed the initial concepts, you may want to see the final choice taken to another level beyond the rough stage, which usually takes the form of a *comprehensive layout.*

A comprehensive layout is a representation that is rendered as closely as possible to the finished product. Once again, there are a number of different terms in use, and there are several levels and kinds of comprehensives.

The differences among comprehensives are based on technique. Some comprehensives are done with markers. Others are done with scanners, computers, and laser printers. Both techniques look wonderful, of course, but both have their pitfalls too.

First, both techniques can take an enormous amount of time, which costs money. Second, the photos and illustrations depend on the concept, and they probably do not exist yet. So, in spite of how wonderful the comps are, you still will not see an exact copy of the finished piece. If you *do* want to see exact comps, photos, or illustrations, you will be spending extra money just to see some ideas.

Let's take a closer look at the differences between these two layout techniques.

Marker comps require a bit more imagination on the part of the client. The photographs are represented by rough drawings, and the copy be ruled lines. Illustrations are usually indicated as loose renderings, not in the final technique that may be utilized. It is usually difficult to duplicate exact printed pieces with marker comps, but they are great for a demonstration of an idea beyond the thumbnails.

Comps done on the computer (usually seen as prints of the file), on the other hand, are great for the client who has difficulty visualizing the end product. Nevertheless, the comp may be misleading. Unless the photographs have already been taken, the copy finalized, and the illustrations completed, the comp is merely a *representation* of what the layout will look like.

In other words, what you see may still not be what you get! And there are some things that the computer can't do yet, such as embossing or printing light solid colors on dark textured paper. If you really need to, you can even have that done before you go to press. Your comp can be as accurate as your pockets are deep.

Be aware, though, unless the color is very accurate (and the more accurate the proof, the more it costs), the images and colors will not be the same as in the final printed piece. There is a wide range of color printers on the market, from inexpensive inkjet printers that do not represent accurate color to very expensive but fairly accurate systems that can simulate the final very closely (e.g., Iris™ prints).

Regardless of the printer, all of these prints are made directly from the original file *before* any film is made. They are used as a tool for viewing on paper the artwork that appears on the computer screen. They are not to be confused with the proofs described in Chapter 11 that are used for checking the film.

Indeed, money saved on elaborate presentations that have a life measured in hours can be better spent elsewhere. Perhaps more important, the creative concept that can be communicated in the simplest possible way is almost always a concept of great power and impact. Ultimately, it will be more understandable to the target audience for the message and more likely will have high memorability and long-term sticking power. And that's what you are looking for, isn't it?

If the idea is right and good, you will see it, and it will fly. If the idea is poor, no amount of elaborate presentation will make it better.

CHAPTER 10

Bringing Ideas to Life:
The Process of Art Production

Developing and polishing a creative concept until it evolves into the heavy weaponry that will do the job for you is undeniably the most difficult—and most enjoyable—part of any project. But make no mistake, there are still plenty of obstacles to hurdle, decisions to make, and fun to have.

The process that takes great ideas to their finished form is called *production.* You may be doing a brochure, an advertising campaign, or format, or a new logo—it still has to be made ready to reproduce. And all of the disciplines that come into play fall under the heading of production.

Photography and illustration are part of that. Perhaps hiring models or food stylists is, too. So are typography and what's known as production art, the human-mechanical process of bringing all these diverse elements together into a form that is ready to be reproduced.

Photography or Illustration?

Whether to use photography or illustration (artwork from any of a variety of sources) depends on the nature of the piece you are doing. Photography is generally more realistic; illustration can be more fanciful.

There are maybe fifty other variables that come into play in making this choice. The following are among the prominent ones:

- Are the products or people to be depicted available for photography? What is the end use? Even though newspaper reproduction is far better than it used to be, a simple line drawing will probably reproduce better than a photo, especially in smaller space units. Check what supermarkets use in their promotions.

- Does what you're depicting lend itself to photography, or could a well-crafted illustration show it off better? Some things in life are, after all, just plain ugly, and a camera's lens is unforgiving.

- What is the cost of using each one? There may be significant dollar savings involved in using one medium instead of the other.

Most often the choice between photography and illustration is fairly obvious, and your designer or art director will recommend the appropriate medium to use. Designers and artists are seldom ambivalent about their choice. Whichever way you go, there are things you should know.

The Art of Photography

If you have chosen to use photography, you still have several decisions to make. Do you hire a photographer or do you use a stock photo supplier? Do you shoot on location or in a studio? Should you use professional models? Do you order black and white prints or color transparencies? As you can see, each decision spawns even more questions.

Most of these decisions are preordained by the nature of your product and by the creative concept itself. Choosing the photographer is easy: let your creative people use the one with whom they are comfortable. It's their responsibility to carry out the project and make it work, and it's hardly fair to make them work with a photographer not of their choosing.

As with selecting other suppliers, though, you can and should ask for at least two competitive bids from equally competent professionals.

Occasionally, there will be a client who thinks photography may be a good place to save money. This isn't true. Using a professional is cheap insurance. Friends who take great vacation photos and dabble in photography are rarely a good substitute for an experienced pro. Indeed, we know of instances in which a good photographer has saved the day due to his or her experience and expertise. Moreover, photographs that are marginally suitable for reproduction can affect the final outcome of a printed piece. It is costly, and often impossible, to fix a bad photograph.

The art director or designer must always attend a photo shoot to direct the photographer regarding angles, cropping, lighting, and myriad other details. True, you can save another couple hundred dollars here, and a good photographer can always "shoot the layout," but this is truly false economy.

In addition, you or someone representing you must also be on hand. For one thing, you should see how hard these professionals work to get the shot just right. For another, something might come up requiring product or technical knowledge that only the client has.

Materials, Products, and Props

Whether you will be shooting on location or in the photographer's studio is another question that will likely be resolved by the creative concepts. Either way, make sure all items to be photographed are in excellent condition.

Colors should be correct, and there should be no scratches or dents or imperfections whatsoever. When doing a series of ads and brochures for a large lock manufacturer, we noticed that there were tiny scratches near the keyhole of many of the locks.

No one at the client company had ever noticed these little marks, but we knew they would show poorly in the finished pieces for these products.

The client was mystified and tracked the problem all the way back to quality control. It seems there's a worker at the end of the production line whose job it is to make sure every lock has the right key. To do this, she inserts and withdraws keys so fast the movement is literally a blur. In the process, the key often made infinitesimal cuts in the keyhole. The problem was resolved by obtaining a lock from the production line before the key-testing station. It was a lot cheaper to delay the shoot a few hours than it would have been to retouch several dozen color transparencies.

Before the shoot, you should be sure to review the layouts for which the photographs will be taken to ensure that all necessary materials, products, and props will be available. Whatever will be required should ideally be delivered to the photo studio (or location site) a day before the shoot, if possible. Then have someone drop by with the list of materials and make sure they are all there.

On-Site Photo Sessions

When photographs will be taken—regardless of whether the site location is yours, a customer's or a vendor's—make sure the shoot is scheduled in advance and that even the lowliest broom-pusher knows about it. It is difficult to shoot around workers who are not prepared for the intrusion of a photo crew. There are also people who simply do not want to be in a picture. Find out who they are and excuse them from being involved. For willing participants, however, make sure the workers are dressed neatly and equipped properly. If they are to wear company shirts or lab coats or hardhats, make sure everything and everyone are perfect.

We once did a capabilities brochure for a manufacturing company whose insurance company required all workers to wear safety glasses. Nobody mentioned this to us, so we really didn't notice that hardly any workers wore the glasses.

Apparently, the company didn't care at the time, but an official did later when the photographs were reviewed. There was not only hell to pay, but also a much larger photography bill.

Expenses

Photography costs vary according to the individual and the rates he or she commands. Most photographers work on a day rate and have a half-day minimum charge. Some include the use of their studio and certain equipment in the rate; others have a base rate covering their services and additional charges for what is used. Some are flexible; others are not. If you plan ahead, you can schedule photo shoots in the most cost-effective way possible. For example, even if you're shooting in color and don't think you'll need black and whites have them shot anyway. It is only pennies now compared to setting up another shoot later.

Additional Members of the Photo Team

There is more to photography than taking pictures. Your product or creative concept may require another kind of expertise on the shoot. For example, if you are showing food, whether as the product or as background, you will need a *food stylist* to make it look the way it should. Food stylists are the people (usually trained as home economists) who can make a hot dog look like a banquet, and they can make some foods look far better than they do in real life. They know all the tricks, such as using glycerine for water droplets, or shaving cream for whipped cream.

If you are using models, professional makeup artists will ensure that the models look perfect on film. They watch for every detail from a shiny nose to a creased collar.

Mr. Murphy and his law guarantee you that if there is a flaw, it will show up on film. Retouching is far more expensive—and far less effective—than being properly prepared at the front end.

While it is tempting for many clients on a limited budget to try to do without this kind of extra cost, in the long run the $500-a-day makeup stylist is far more economical than the $1,500 retouching job.

If your concept calls for models, there is the decision of whether to go with expensive professionals (plus the agent's commission) or to enlist people from your company. Working in front of a camera is hard work, and doing it exceptionally well requires a very special talent. It is not as easy as it looks to appear relaxed and natural, to pose without looking stiff, and to react to the camera rather than stand stiffly in front of it.

The decision to use nonprofessionals should be determined by the importance of the people in the photograph. If they are needed for background or atmosphere, you can probably get along fine without professionals. (This and other decisions will not be a surprise to you at this point, because you have long ago considered models—and stylists and makeup persons—as a line item in your budget planning worksheet. Figure 4.2, Chapter 4.)

Rights and Ownership

The last but not least important issue to consider when using photography involves rights. When you or your agent are dealing with a commercial photographer, make sure everybody is aware of the ground rules for the use and reuse of the photographs. Many photographers do not turn over the original negatives or transparencies to their clients. Some will provide duplicate transparencies (of whatever format is best for the job, usually 4 × 5 35mm or 2¼) and an original print from color negative film for a *specifically defined use.*

In other words, you may not have ownership of the photographs, you may only have their use for a certain purpose (e.g., one advertisement, one brochure, or one catalog). If you wish to use the image again in another way, you may have to get permission from the photographer and pay an additional use fee. By the same token, you should be able to restrict the photographer's own use of the photographs that he or she took for you.

Most often, the photographers who operate that way are the ones with day rates so high you will probably not be using them anyway. But their quality and professionalism may be worth the fee. It's your call.

Stock Photos

In our work, we are accustomed to engaging professional photographers who shoot great pictures; get paid fairly and promptly for their talent, equipment, and overhead; and then giving our client full rights to the film purchased from the photographer.

If some or all of your needs are generic (e.g., pictures of flowers) you can be well served by use of *stock* (library) photos. Stock photo libraries exist in all major markets. They usually have catalogs of subject matter ranging from apples to zebras and almost everything in between:

scenes, machinery, old cars, backgrounds, babies, women in kitchens, men in kitchens, you name it.

Stock photos are leased to you on a per-use basis. A photo used in a brochure with a print run of 1,000 will be charged at minimum rate. The same photo used in a national ad campaign, a brochure, and billboards will be charged at a much higher rate.

You may wonder about the difference between the photographer who wants to be paid by the use and the stock photo house that is paid per use. In our opinion, it's the photographer's business to take pictures and it's the stock house's business to rent them. It all goes back to ownership, and the copyright laws protect those who are the creators.

But don't think stock photos are the skinflint's way out. They can be quite expensive, and you have little exclusivity protection. While it is not likely that you and a competitor would use the same photo in your brochures, it has happened.

The Art of Illustration

The styles and techniques of illustration are as broad and diverse as art itself, from simple line drawings to elaborate color paintings. Many illustrations can now be done on the computer, but as with most machines, the end result is only as good and as artistic as the person operating the machine.

Charts and graphs, for example, are items that can be done fairly well with computers. And all we know for sure is, what can be done fairly well today will most likely be done very well tomorrow.

Nevertheless, computers and their programs are not sensitive, not thoughtful, not imaginative. These are the qualities a good illustrator brings to the table, in addition to the ability to translate an idea into a dynamic piece of artwork.

Other types of illustrations frequently used in marketing communications pieces are cartoons, airbrush or watercolor renderings, cutaways (cross-sections that show the complex insides of something), paper sculptures (and those in other media, such as the Claymation® figures that became such popular symbols for the California raisin industry), and even tapestries woven with a corporate logo.

Illustrations are subject to similar ownership and usage rules as photography. Be sure whether you are buying full rights (you own it and you use it however, whenever, and wherever you want, forever) or limited use (for a defined period and a specific project).

All rights are negotiable, of course, but they must be determined up front! Try to anticipate all of your usage needs and offer a package price. Whatever you do, *do not ever think* of reproducing an illustration or a photograph without permission of the illustrator or photographer.

We have had clients snip drawings out of magazines and ask that they be used in their own brochure. No. Not even if you think the originator will never see the piece. Things have a habit of turning up in the strangest places.

The Art of Production Art

Numerous interchangeable terms fall under the heading of production art: *camera-ready art, mechanical art* (or simply, *mechanicals*), *production art,* even *keylining and pasteup,* although that is falling into disuse in this computer age.

All these terms mean pretty much the same thing, and they all include the following elements:

• Typeset copy

• Photography or illustration (sometimes both)

• Fancy borders or other design elements

• Company and/or product logotypes

Working from the final approved layout, the production artist assembles all the required components and positions them in the exact size and place they will appear in the finished product.

A look at the steps involved in doing the final artwork will help you understand how each piece comes together. There are two ways the artwork can be created, either traditionally with art boards or on the computer. However, you will achieve higher quality at equal or lower prices if the work is done on computer.

The Traditional Approach *(for Those with Computer Phobias)*

In the "old" days before computers began taking over, no artist could exist without a glue-pot or waxer, an illustration board, a T square, and a knife. The artist spent hours—sometimes days or even months— leaning over a drawing board with a T square, pasting the components on illustration board (hence the term *pasteup*) to get a piece of artwork ready to go to the printer.

Although the tools used today are quite different and the methods are sometimes faster, the principles of doing mechanicals remain the same. By understanding what the pieces are and how they need to come together in traditional "pasteups" (Figure 10.1), the step to computer-generated art will seem less complicated.

STEP 1: The artist sizes the typewritten copy by counting the number of characters and using a formula to determine how it will fit into the layout. He or she indicates the size and type style (typeface or font) by marking instructions on the original typewritten copy.

STEP 2: The copy is typeset and provided in *galley* form (blocks of type on sheets of reproduction-quality white paper) by a typesetting company.

STEP 3: The illustration board is taped to the drawing board and prepared. At the top, bottom, and sides are inked lines, called *crop marks,* to indicate the outer limits of the ad or page and to mark where the piece will be trimmed. Margins and other important measurements may be ruled with nonreproducible blue pen or pencil.

STEP 4: The galleys are glued and cut into pieces. Each piece is pasted in the appropriate spot within the crop marks.

STEP 5: Photos, illustrations, or other materials with tonal values (i.e., lights and darks, called *continuous tones*), are indicated in the assembly by *position-only* reproductions of the originals. The reproductions are to exact scale, either enlarged or reduced as the final layout indicates. The position-only copies are then pasted down on the

Figure 10.1 Creating Artwork on Art Boards

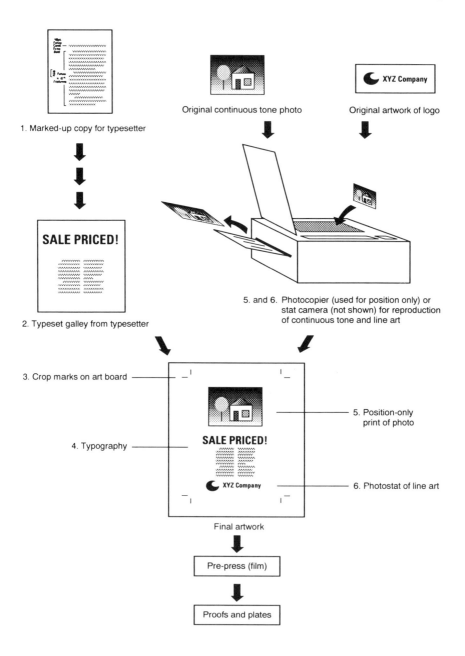

1. Marked-up copy for typesetter

Original continuous tone photo

Original artwork of logo

2. Typeset galley from typesetter

5. and 6. Photocopier (used for position only) or stat camera (not shown) for reproduction of continuous tone and line art

3. Crop marks on art board

4. Typography

5. Position-only print of photo

6. Photostat of line art

Final artwork

Pre-press (film)

Proofs and plates

illustration board, along with the typesetting. (These copies are not reproduced in the final printing. This will be explained later in the description of the pre-press process.)

Sometimes an artist will use a *window* instead of an actual reproduction of the image. The window is a box put in the position of the image. Since red or amber is seen as black by the camera, usually the artist cuts the shape out of special red or amber materials meant specifically for this purpose. The percentage of reduction or enlargement and cropping of that image is indicated on the original; then it is shot and put into position separately in the pre-press process.

STEP 6:   Any *line art* (no tonal values, just black and white), such as logos, borders, or illustrations, are sized. Reproductions (i.e., *photostats*) are made and pasted in position. Unlike position-only reproductions, these will be used in the pre-press process, therefore they need to be very clean.

If more than one color is to be used (for example, the text in black, the headline in blue, and the company logo in red), clear acetate overlays may be used for the materials in each color. Usually, anything to be printed in black is pasted on the board directly. The scaled reproductions of the continuous tone elements mentioned above are also pasted onto the board itself.

The entire board is covered with a protective tissue on which are written the instructions to the printer (for a brochure) or the color separator or film-maker (for ads).

Now that we have outlined the basic steps, let's go back and examine how the client and other members of the creative team fit into the process. Regardless of whether the traditional or computerized method is used to create the piece, one rule remains true: The later in the process that corrections and changes are made, the more expensive those corrections and changes will be.

Whenever you are given the opportunity to review the copy and the photography or illustrations, take your task very seriously. Read and examine everything carefully. Mistakes that are caught in the early stages of production are much easier and less expensive to remedy than those caught later on. After you have read the same copy many times, you may wish to enlist the proofreading services of a colleague. Fresh eyes are more likely to spot errors. Even if you completely trust the members of your creative team, they will not be aware of changes made within your organization that may affect the accuracy of the text. It is your responsibility to read the text, examine the art and photographs, and ensure that all the elements are accurate and up-to-date.

Usually before the art boards are sent to the printer, the client has a final chance to see the artwork and text. It is very important to make any corrections or revisions at this point. Changes can be indicated either on the tissues or on a photocopy of the artwork.

Removing and replacing pasted-down elements, reordering type, or resizing images all takes time. And time—you guessed it—translates into money. So make sure you approve the copy *before* type is ordered and approve the images *before* they are sized.

But mistakes do happen and minds do change. So let everybody see the boards who needs to, make the corrections, and then proofread the revisions carefully. Whatever you do, please don't show the boards to anyone but people with approval power (unless you know their proofing skills are invaluable). This isn't the time to rethink the concept or change the images.

One important word about approvals. At this point you should be asked to sign the text and artwork, stating that they are approved or approved with indicated revisions. If revisions are made, you should sign again once the boards are perfect. After you sign, you are responsible—even if you missed a typographical error that wasn't your fault. Your signature means that you accept the work as is and that it can go to film. So read carefully.

The Computerized Method

Alas, this time-honored method of producing art boards is in real danger of extinction, replaced by the whir of a computer. Using a desktop publishing or drawing program, the production artist does all the assembly with the machine's bits and bytes.

Figure 10.2   Creating Artwork on a Computer

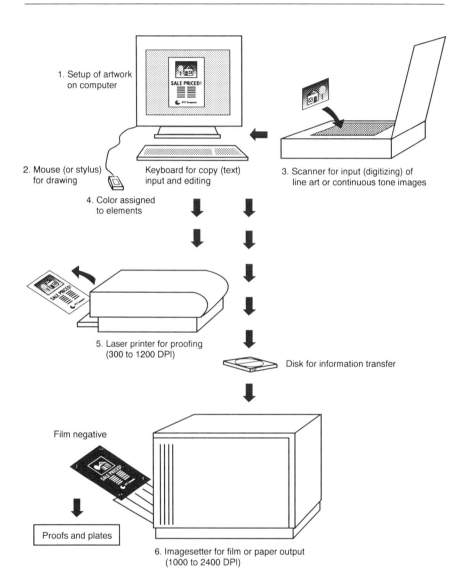

1. Setup of artwork
   on computer

2. Mouse (or stylus)
   for drawing

   Keyboard for copy (text)
   input and editing

3. Scanner for input (digitizing) of
   line art or continuous tone images

4. Color assigned
   to elements

5. Laser printer for proofing
   (300 to 1200 DPI)

Disk for information transfer

Film negative

Proofs and plates

6. Imagesetter for film or paper output
   (1000 to 2400 DPI)

Although the tools are quite different, the steps are similar. The elements don't change; they only manifest themselves in different ways. Look at figures 10.1 and 10.2 to compare the two methods.

Now let's take a look at the steps used by the computer artist to assemble the artwork.

STEP 1: The document is set up in a desktop publishing or art program with crop marks and text blocks. The text can either be imported from a word processing program or typed directly into the publishing program. The artist assigns the type styles and sizes to all the text.

STEP 2: Any line art elements (i.e., logos, drawings, or borders)— brought in from a drawing program, clip art files, or scans of the originals—are placed in the document.

STEP 3: A service bureau or printer (the vendor who will ultimately print the final copies) prepares a high-resolution scan of each continuous tone image. As resolution increases, so does the amount of memory used on the computer; consequently, the scans are provided in a low-resolution format to the artist. (The higher the resolution, the better the quality of the scan. Although desktop scanners are adequate, they are not meant for quality work.) The artist then places the scanned images into the document.

STEP 4: The artist assigns color to the various elements. Any artwork that is created outside the document usually has the color assigned before it is imported.

STEP 5: Laser proofs are made. This is the point where the client can come in an make changes most economically. The advantage of the computer over the keyline and pasteup method becomes very apparent during this step. It is much easier to see all the pieces come together on a laser proof than it is on a board with layers of acetate and tissues. It is also much easier to make changes on a computer than it is to do new typesetting, new pasteups, or new illustrations in other colors. This would also be the stage whcrc color prints can be made, if required. (Again, this is an expensive and usually unnecessary option and is only used as a preview, not to proof final color.)

You will be asked to sign the final laser proofs that reflect all changes and corrections. This sign-off is your assumption of responsibility for the piece.

STEP 6: Once the lasers are signed off, the document and all the related imported files are saved to a disk and given to the service bureau or printer, along with the laser proofs and instructions. Film can then be made directly from the disk.

Some artists still prefer providing an art board, even though the work was done on computer. In that case, the artwork is output to a high-quality paper at a high resolution and the artist mounts it on a board with glue or wax. Color breaks are then designated in the traditional manner. The film is made from a camera shot of the boards, and all photos are stripped in separately, following the same process as that of traditional pasteups.

All this electronic wizardry does not eliminate the need for the production artist to arrange all the elements in the same manner as with traditional pasteup. In fact, the time involved is sometimes greater than it is in the old method of sending copy to a specialist for typesetting, then pasting everything down.

In this computer age, the production artist becomes the typesetter, too, and must focus on the special discipline of making the typography the design element it is—as well as not making any typos (typographical errors).

In the old days of rubber-cemented pasteups, even the sloppiest piece of mechanical art could be cleaned up somewhat (even more than somewhat) in the next stage of production (pre-press), which is the making of the film negatives by the printer, the magazine or newspaper, or the specialized business that only makes film. And many times those old pros have saved somebody's bacon by repairing botched artwork and finding mistakes that nobody else found.

But today's computer artists have to know almost as much about how film is made and how it affects the printing as the pro in the back room. They are no longer creative people with some production skills. They have become production people with creative ability. This new breed can be dangerous if they totally operate from the right side of the brain. That is why there are art directors and production artists! However, if you find someone who is equally knowledgeable and talented in art as well as production, that is someone you want to hold on to.

So, let me repeat something I said earlier, please leave the preparation of artwork to the pros, unless you want to learn more about printing than you'll ever learn in this book.

CHAPTER 11

Getting Ready for the Printer:

Pre-press Production

You can skip this chapter and still be pretty shrewd about advertising and brochures and all the other things in which you involve yourself. The pre-press process is quite technical and is often confusing to people who are not in the graphic-arts business, as well as to some who are. Pre-press is the stage between the preparation of production art and the final process of printing a brochure or an ad. All other things being equal, consummate work at this stage probably will not even be noticed. But poor work could ruin or cripple your entire project.

This is the point where the production art we prepared in Chapter 10 gets translated into the finished product that comes off the press in Chapter 13.

In pre-press, the production art is transformed into a photographic negative that is used to make the plates that will be used to print your project.

The pre-press work can be done by color trade houses, service bureaus, in-house departments, or printers. Let's examine each one separately.

Color trade houses also make the film negatives for black and white publications and do work for printers that do not have their own facilities.

Their prices are sometimes higher than those of some other sources, because they have the best and latest equipment and the people who know how to run it. On the other hand, there are some houses that are saddled with a major investment in equipment that they purchased several years ago, which is neither state-of-the-art nor cost-effective. Their pricing may be low, just to keep the work coming in the door and the payments met.

Service bureaus are a relative newcomer to the mix. They are often typesetters who have sought new profit centers as computers and programs enable increasingly more ad agencies and design firms to do their own work in-house. Service bureaus usually own some expensive film-making equipment, but sometimes the staff members don't have the knowledge or experience to produce film for the increasingly bewildering array of printing presses, each with its own peculiarities and needs for film negatives.

Service bureaus are improving though, as more people are being trained. If you are concerned, it's a good idea to ask your printer about his or her experience with the film provided by a particular bureau. Don't spend the money first and find out later.

If your needs are limited, and you only need a vendor to produce linotronic output to paper or basic film, a service bureau is your place. In fact, most service bureaus are now equipped with some form of pre-film proofing system (directly from the computer file). These proofs vary greatly in accuracy, so be sure to ask how good they are.

In-house departments are rare except in large companies with a high volume of graphic-arts work. These usually have the same problem as service bureaus: lots of good gear, not enough good people.

Printers. It makes sense to have the company that will be printing your work also do the pre-press if it has the proper equipment. Most large- and medium-size printers do. If yours doesn't, have them subcontract the pre-press work. It shouldn't cost you any more because the printer will get a trade price. More important, he or she becomes responsible for the quality of the film negatives and cannot blame someone else if the job isn't right.

The Illustrated Guide to Pre-press

Regardless of who handles the pre-press work for your project, the steps will be the same (Figure 11.1). First let's take a look at the steps when following the traditional method based on art boards rather than computer-generated art.

STEP 1: The art board is photographed by a camera (hence the term *camera-ready*) that shoots only the line art (i.e., the type, borders, charts, etc.). These are all solids with no shades of gray—no tonal values, as discussed in Chapter 10. (If artwork is prepared with a computer and an appropriate printer, film can be output directly and this step can be skipped.)

STEP 2: Color photographs or illustrations—materials with tonal values—are run through the scanner and converted to dots. The more dots per inch, the finer the "line screen" and the greater the quality of reproduction. (A newspaper screen might have 85 dots per inch; magazines, 120 or 133; and a fine coffee-table art book, 300 or more. The line screen used will depend on the type of press and paper being used.)

STEP 3: The color images are then converted into *separations,* one piece of film for each of the four colors used in four-color printing: cyan, magenta, yellow, and black. Each color has a different dot pattern. When the four are layered onto one another in sequence, the original image appears. Simply put, four-color process printing combines the four process ink colors to make other colors. It is the only method that can be used to reproduce photographs or illustrations.

STEP 4: Black and white continuous-tone images are converted into *halftones* by a different camera than the one used in Step 1 for line art. Again, the image is converted into dots. Usually, halftones or color images are square or rectangular, but designers also use variations such as outlines (no background) or vignettes (a soft edge around the image). These nonconventional processes cost more.

Figure 11.1 Creating Film and Proofs (Pre-press)

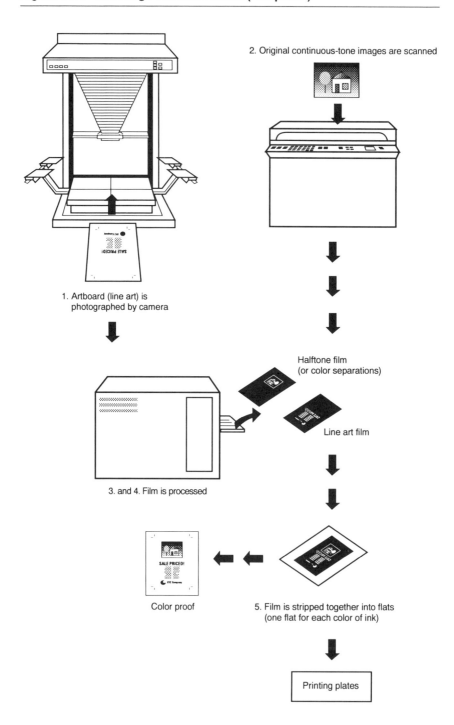

2. Original continuous-tone images are scanned

1. Artboard (line art) is photographed by camera

Halftone film (or color separations)

Line art film

3. and 4. Film is processed

Color proof

5. Film is stripped together into flats (one flat for each color of ink)

Printing plates

STEP 5: The next step is to make proofs of the color film. But first it is important to understand the difference between creating film from computer-generated art and the time-honored fashion of shooting art boards and images with a camera, as described above.

In Chapter 10 you learned that scanned images may be imported into the piece as low-resolution scans if the artwork is done on computer. Now those scans are replaced by the printer or service bureau with high-resolution images in the same document as the line art. At the same time, the line screens are assigned. The best part is that it is done automatically by the computer. Since the artwork prepared on computer is completely assembled *before* the film is output, the film comes out as one piece for each color of ink with all the pieces in place.

With artwork that is prepared traditionally, the line film made in Step 1 and the tone film in Steps 2 and 4 are combined to make a *flat.* A flat is made by *stripping* (cutting with a knife) together all the pieces of film on a light table, as one large piece. Each separate color of ink requires a separate flat.

The good news is that hours can be saved by assembling everything on a computer. The flat is practically completed on the computer before a single blade has been dulled the traditional way. The bad news is that the fine craftspeople called *strippers,* who do the assembly work by hand, are a dying breed. They have the ability to do some amazing tricks to save flawed film, simply by using a brush, opaqing material, and a knife. Nowadays you will find many of these talented folks retrained as operators of the very sophisticated equipment that makes the film from the computer-generated art. As more emphasis is placed on the artist to do the pre-press work that the strippers used to do, many of these operators are still saving flawed work; they are just using different tools on different media.

Checking the Film

There are essentially three tools used for checking that the film is accurate: *color proofs, bluelines,* and *color keys.* Each serves a different purpose, but each is equally valuable in assuring that the printed piece is, in fact, what appeared in the artwork. (Remember, you made sure that the artwork was exactly what you wanted before the film was made, when you signed the approval.)

If you are dealing with color, especially four color, an item called a *contact proof* shows you, within certain limitations of the process, what the final, printed color will look like. (These proofs have several trade names—Fujiprint, Matchprint, Chromalin, and Waterproof are some; in this book we will use contact proof.) The proofs cost a little extra, but they are usually pretty inexpensive insurance for a first-class job. You will see proofs that look much like color prints from the camera store, except they are the size they will appear in your finished piece. If you look at them carefully with a special glass, called a *loop,* you will see a dot pattern.

Contact proofs are made to assure that the fidelity of the color artwork has been faithfully translated from the original to the printing negatives. Usually the artist will tell the production house up front that he or she either wants the final image to match the original as closely as possible or to adjust the color a bit.

Each photo or color illustration can be proofed individually, not in position on the page, or as a *composite proof* with all the other elements combined on the page. Either way, the proof is made by exposing the film for each color, one on top of the other, to a special paper or to the actual press sheet. The image will appear as the closest representation possible of an offset proof without putting ink to paper.

You will find that printers will vary in the type of proof they provide. Many always insist on loose proofs being made before a composite is done. Others, trying to transition to the newer world of computer-generated art, prefer composite proofs.

The checking of color proofs may be one of the areas that you should refer to your artist. There are many variables in reproducing color images, and a trained professional will know what is acceptable and what is not, based on the technical specifications and the capabilities of the proofing process employed. Consider this example: the best four-color images are reproduced from original transparencies. They are usually viewed on a light box, with the light going all the way through them.

That light is difficult, at best, to capture on the printed page, even with the best laser scanner. Paper is not transparent, so it reflects the light; therefore, it never allows for the same brightness as the image seen on the light box. The pros know how to adjust for this dilemma and make the best of the situation.

Finally, many separators allow for one or two corrections to color for each separation. When you or the artist starts asking for more, you had better be sure that (a) the film really can be improved, and (b) your pockets are deep. The key is to be reasonable about your expectations and to know up front the level of quality to expect from your supplier. I have seen color separators get the color perfect on the first pass and others never get it right. This is just another area to remember to cover in your contract.

The *blueline* (which goes by many names) is your last chance to check a job for errors. This proof shows you how well the printer has made the negatives. It should look exactly the way the piece will look when it is printed in terms of content. The proof itself may have a blue tint and the paper is coated and treated with chemicals. Your job is to read all of the copy once again and make sure it's all there and there isn't a typographical error lurking anywhere. Also check the positioning of all the elements, the trim, the fold, and the pagination. Look for strange flecks (dirt on the film) or missing pieces. The creative team will have done the same.

Nevertheless, the importance of checking the bluelines carefully can't be stressed enough. More than one artist has accidentally given a printer an older version of an art file. And more than one printer has stripped the wrong photo above the wrong caption. I've even seen one half of a photo missing on the bluelines; the stripper had inadvertently cut the image without realizing it.

The changes you make on the bluelines will result in significantly high charges, so evaluate whether the change is really worth it. Usually, at this stage, only the most glaring errors and oversights warrant correction. The fine-tuning should have been done much earlier. On the other hand, any errors you have found that were made after you approved the laser proofs or art boards should be picked up by the guilty party.

As much as I hate to admit it, I have bought new film for clients and I have seen printers completely absorb the cost of new film because of their errors. The quality people, clients included, know and admit when they have made a mistake.

The blueline proof is not the place to check for color or quality of the images. Not only is the proof not in color, but also the bluelines are often poor reproductions of the film. Sometimes one page will even look lighter or darker than another. On the other hand, the same film is used to make the composite proof mentioned in Step 5, so color can be checked very closely in the contact proof.

Your final job is to sign the little piece of paper attached to the blueline stating that it is either "OK as is" or "OK with changes as noted." There is also a place where you can request a second blueline reflecting the changes you made.

You will also notice that there is a little line of type that says you accept full responsibility for any errors in the final printed piece and that you agree to pay any charges resulting from changes made after this approval. As a result, most of us look at bluelines very carefully.

Last, there is the antiquated proof that you may rarely see, called a *color key,* a manufactured proof that is made by exposing each flat of film, by color, to a specially treated acetate proofing material. When the layers are all combined one on top of the other, the final images appear as they will when printed in color. This proof is only used to check the position of elements, color breaks, and overall appearance, not color accuracy. Many publications still require color keys in order to match the dots and color breaks for each piece of film to the final printed piece. This form of proofing, however, is becoming extinct as increasingly more work is done on the computer.

These three proofs—the contact proof, the blueline, and the color key—should be the last time changes are made. Any changes made to the artwork at this point—such as rearranging elements, substituting photos, or changing colors—will result in considerably higher charges.

Signing off on these proofs means that you are accepting the film as it is, or as you and the supplier have agreed to change it. Before any agreements to change are made, you know how much the cost will be.

If a problem surfaces later, it will be your error—and your cost for fixing it. It gets *very* expensive to make changes after this point.

So, be careful. (I can't say that too often.) *Review everything slowly and methodically* before signing off on the work. Don't be reluctant to ask neophyte questions. It's your job. And don't be intimidated by a ticking clock or a twitchy technician. As a practical matter, the art director or designer who created the production piece will be checking the color accuracy and other technical details.

The bottom line is that the entire project is your responsibility. As they say in the printing industry, "No whining after signing."

After the proofs have been signed off, printing plates are made, transferring the image from the film to a light-sensitive alloy by laser beam.

As this book is being written, digital and direct-to-plate printing are advancing rapidly toward full development. With digital printing, the film and plate stages will ultimately be eliminated and the product will be made directly from the information stored in the computer. With direct-to-plate printing, images are transferred directly to the printing plates, with no film being used. Proofs are made right from the press to the paper.

Ben Franklin wouldn't recognize printing today!

Dabbling in Colors

You may go your entire career without being involved in a complex, expensive four-color project such as the one we've just discussed. Most printed materials and most ads are in good old black and white, with a splash of another color for emphasis.

Frequently, these other colors are not made by the complicated four-color process. They're made by blending inks, exactly the same way the clerk at the hardware store blends paint.

When designing a piece, the artist can specify the exact color to be used, and that color can be matched precisely by the printer or, in the case of ads, by publications offering color printing (for a charge, of course).

What makes it possible is the Pantone Matching System™ (PMS). Artists use books with thousands of swatches of PMS colors, each one numbered, to get exactly the color they want for, say, a company logo.

So, as a quick review, the four-color process is the combination of the inks cyan, magenta, yellow, and black. By laying one on top of the other with screens of the image to be printed, millions of other colors can be achieved. When looked at through a magnifying glass, you can see the dots in these combined colors. This method is used for reproducing color photos or illustrations with tonal values.

PMS, on the other hand, uses inks (as opposed to dots) to achieve color. It is used in areas where solid or a percentage of a single, specific color is required or where a second color is added to a black and white photo. Designers sometimes use PMS colors alone for photos, but it usually is to achieve a specific effect.

PMS colors cannot generally be mixed from the four-color process inks if an exact match is required. However, printers can refer to a formula of screen mixes to try and simulate them. If it is critical that your PMS color be matched perfectly on a process job, pay for the extra plate and printing. You may be disappointed otherwise.

Although the Pantone Matching System dominates the printing industry, new ones are popping up regularly. Many printers are turning to competitors, but the Pantone people are always keeping up with the trends, thus staying as the leader.

A recent newcomer to printing is the soy-based ink. Usually, inks have an oil base, resulting in detrimental effects on the environment. Although soy-based inks still have environmental consequences, they are manufactured from a renewable resource; therefore, they are sometimes more desirable.

Whatever the design requires, the artist must clearly describe to the printer the colors that will be used, by either PMS number or four-color process. Of course, PMS colors and four-color process are commonly combined on one piece of artwork. To reproduce such a job for the best quality and maximum cost-effectiveness, it would be worthwhile to talk to your printer and find out what type of press will be used. If the job will be four color plus one PMS, it may be worthwhile to use a five- or six-color press and run all the inks at once. The alternative would be to run on a four-color press with the process colors, then going back through the press for the PMS plate. The decision depends on the quantity and sheet size and hourly rates of the different presses.

Some Words to the Wise

Now that you know the fundamentals of the pre-press work, you need a few pointers on selecting the pre-press supplier. (These suppliers were described at the beginning of this chapter.)

You may consider letting the printer decide who will do the pre-press work. Unless you are very confident that a specific supplier's pre-press work will be suitable and acceptable to the printer (and you), let the printer worry about it.

I have seen many a client caught in a catch-22 situation with the printer blaming problems on the pre-press supplier and the pre-press supplier blaming the printer. And guess who is stuck in the middle.

There are many factors in creating good film, and missing any one of them can make or break a job. The film must be prepared accurately to suit the press that will print the job, the scans need to be perfect, the color must be right, and the stripping must be exact.

Most pre-press people want to do quality work. If you or your artist has all the confidence in the world that a supplier's film will be perfect, there is no need to be concerned. If you have any hesitation at all, let the printer take the responsibility. Then the printer is in control, responsible for the successes, as well as the messes.

CHAPTER 12

Selecting and Working with Printers

As with everything else, you have to compare apples to apples before you can make an intelligent choice regarding a printer. If you're not experienced in buying printing, the creative resource working with you certainly should be.

If you're on familiar ground, you will know what type of printer is right for the work you are doing. You will match the requirements of the job to the capabilities of the printer and his or her equipment. You can get bids on the work and go for it.

If you are breaking into new territory here, you will have to rely on the expertise of your creative resources. Since you have faithfully followed the advice in this book, you have every confidence in them. However, keep your oar in the water during this vital part of the project. Ask to talk to the printer's sales representatives yourself, because they are the people who will shepherd your project through the shop, making sure everything goes the way you want it to. Ask for an equipment list, even if you don't know a Miehle 8375 from a Peterbilt truck. Ask to see samples of the printer's work that are similar to yours. Also, don't be reluctant to ask for a tour of the plant. All plants stink of ink, but the proper shop will be clean enough for open-heart surgery.

You have to get to know the level of standards for the printer(s) you use. You may pay a few more centimes for the attention paid to the details, such as keeping the place spotless, but it will be worth it.

There are a lot of printers in this world. But for your work-in-progress, cut the squad down to three for bidding purposes. After you and your team have narrowed the field, prepare a specification sheet (Figure 12.1).

Your specifications will include a brief description of the piece to be printed, quantity, finished size, number of pages, weight and type of paper (by name), number of inks, number of photographs, size of photos, delivery, sales tax, and any other special instructions that might affect the pricing.

This form forces you to give each printer identical specifications. Whenever you can give three printers of comparable quality an identical set of specs for any given job, you can feel completely confident about choosing the lowest bidder. However, if the printers differ at all in quality, capability, or service, be careful of basing your decision on numbers alone.

Let's take a moment to address the issue of comparable quality. Many of you have a printer you feel good about. You know that you will get adequate quality at the price you want. Nevertheless, quality and price are not the only considerations when comparing printers.

Even though I encourage the "three-bids" approach, having a great working relationship with one or two printers is certainly acceptable. You will most likely be given a little extra attention on rush jobs or better buys on paper when they can be passed on. Your printer should work with you so that the job is run as cost-effectively as possible. But don't expect discounts. Even your good working relationship isn't enough to cut the printer's profit margin even lower.

You need to be aware of your printer's limitations and the situation for which somebody else might be better suited. Some buyers have a stable of six or seven good printers, each with its own area of specialization. They may have one printer for the hurry-up, small run, one- or two-color jobs. They may have other printers to handle the larger jobs that require more attention, time, and bigger presses. They also may have other printers who are equipped with a variety of presses to meet specialized needs.

The best printer is the one who is honest about his or her niche. I always appreciate it when a printing rep says, "May I recommend XYZ

Figure 12.1   Printer Specification Sheet

Fill out a separate form for each piece.

Company: _____ Date: _____

Contact: _____

Address: _____

Phone: _____ FAX: _____

Printer Name: _____ Contact: _____

Address: _____

Phone: _____ FAX: _____

Job Name: _____ Job No.: _____

Job Description: _____ Date Due: _____

Quantity: 1) _____ 2) _____ 3) _____ Additional/m's: _____

Size: Flat _____ x _____ Folded/Bound _____ x _____

No. of pages: _____ Self-cover _____ Plus cover _____

Art provided as:

    Disk (type) _____ Program _____ Version _____

    Artboard _____

    Composed film with proofs _____ Loose film _____

    Printer to prepare _____

Number of inks: Cover side one _____ Cover side two _____

                   Inside side one _____ Inside side two _____

Special inks and/or varnish: _____

Number of separations and sizes:

    From transparencies _____

    From reflective _____

Figure 12.1   Printer Specification Sheet *(continued)*

Number of halftones and sizes:

Halftones _____

Duotones _____

Photo special effects (mezzotints, line conversions, etc,): _____

_____

Photo alterations (outlines, vignettes, retouch): _____

_____

Stock: Weight   Name   Finish   Color   Grade

Cover   _____   _____   _____   _____   _____

Inside   _____   _____   _____   _____   _____

Fold type: _____

Bindery:

Flat ___ Collate & gather ___ Punch ___ Drill Score/perforate ___

Pad ___ Saddle stitch ___ Paste bind ___ Perfect bind ___ GVC ___

Wire-O ___ Spiral bound ___ Case bound ___ Tip in ___

Special (i.e., emboss, foil, die-cut, number, etc.): _____

_____

Packing instructions: _____

Delivery: _____

Additional information: _____

_____

_____

_____

_____

Printers down the street? We specialize in four-color, large runs (50,000 or more), and I may not be as competitively priced. XYZ has a smaller press and specializes in two-color, quality printing." You can be sure I would come back to that rep when I do have the right job.

Some printers say yes to any request and then farm out the work if they can't handle it. If the quality, price, and schedule don't change, then that is acceptable. However, there is now a middle agent and you are one step farther away from control. Unless you know the subcontractor and trust the printer you hired, avoid this situation.

There are many types and sizes of printing presses, from the one-color baby presses that take a maximum size of 8½" x 11" paper to the building-size web presses. Even though you may not know the specifications of all the presses, you can get a general idea of who does what. Besides, you can be easily fooled if you are choosing by press size alone. The service, pre-press department, press operator, bindery facility, and delivery also take part in creating a quality shop.

The best way to identify the correct printer for you is to make a list of all the printers' capabilities (Figure 12.2), even rating them the way you did when choosing your creative resources. Ask for samples of their work when you tour their facility. Then call the company whose sample you have and ask if you can speak to the person who handled the printing. Ask that person about his or her experience with the printer. After all, the piece may look good to you, but you don't know how painful or pleasant the journey was that led to the delivered piece.

The Printer's Representative

The mid-size and larger firms usually will assign a sales representative to you. Some of these people are worth gold. The good rep will interface with you regarding every phase of the work. Your rep can make production suggestions to save time or money, do some of the running around (of artwork or proofs, for example), and provide hints about deals on paper. In fact, the best reps babysit the job from start to finish. I have followed more than one rep when they changed companies.

If you attend the press checks, your rep should be there also. If you are at all uncertain about what you are looking for, he or she can speak the correct language and make sure your concerns are clear to the production people. I am always amazed at how printing reps function after several days of middle-of-the-night press checks. (Press checks seem to be like the birth of babies, they always happen in the wee hours.) Good printing reps certainly earn their keep.

Sales reps usually work for one company, but every so often you find one who represents two or more printers, just to keep the bases covered. They are on salary or commission and stay faithful to their companies.

Printing brokers, on the other hand, represent a larger spectrum of printers and are usually independent contractors. They are helpful when you don't have the time or energy to obtain competitive bids on a job. The broker knows whom to contact and where to get the best prices. On the other hand, some brokers do not like to reveal their sources, thus keeping you out of the loop.

The Printer's Quotations

I am sometimes amazed at how I can provide identical information to three vendors and receive five variations. As hard as I may try to be clear, there are many fine points that sometimes slip through the cracks. That is why it is helpful to use a request for quotation form, and discuss it with the printers' reps. Their ideas and suggestions can be very helpful, but if you add or change anything, do it for all the competitors.

Occasionally printers get creative without your knowing it. They may price the job on their "house paper" instead of on what you designated, or they may decide to "gang" some separations (that is, scan more than one at a time). These types of changes can affect the level of quality. Make sure you read every line of the estimate.

A pet peeve of mine is the quotation that comes over the phone with no paperwork follow-up. That practice can be revealing about how an operation is run. The typed quotation tells you about the printer before

Figure 12.2 Printer Evaluation Form

Date _____

Name of Company _____

Address _____

_____

Phone _____ FAX _____

Contact _____

Title _____

Type of printer: __ Quick __ Small __ Mid-size __ Large __ Specialty

Rate the following 1-10 (10 = premium or best)

_____ Quality   _____ Pre-press capabilities

_____ Service   _____ Proofing capabilities

_____ Shop appearance   _____ Art department

_____ Reputation   _____ Samples

Sheetfed offset press descriptions:

Brand _____ Max. Sheet Size ____ Min. Sheet Size ____ # Colors ____

Brand _____ Max. Sheet Size ____ Min. Sheet Size ____ # Colors ____

Brand _____ Max. Sheet Size ____ Min. Sheet Size ____ # Colors ____

Brand _____ Max. Sheet Size ____ Min. Sheet Size ____ # Colors ____

Web offset press descriptions:

Brand _____ Maximum Roll Width ____ Cut-off ____ # Colors ____

Brand _____ Maximum Roll Width ____ Cut-off ____ # Colors ____

Additional capabilities (i.e., die cut, foil stamp, embossing, engraving, thermography)

_____

_____

_____

Figure 12.2   Printer Evaluation Form *(continued)*

Area of specialization _____

_____

Describe capabilities, limitations, and equipment available:

Cutting _____

Folding _____

Binding (i.e., wire, saddle stitch, staple, perfect, case, etc.)

_____

_____

Art department _____

_____

Pre-press services _____

_____

Delivery _____

Storage _____

Credit terms _____

Scheduling procedures _____

Previous customer references _____

_____

Comments _____

_____

_____

_____

_____

_____

_____

you even work with him or her. If it is timely, organized, and very clear, then most likely the job will be too.

It is a good idea to ask the printer to break out some of the costs of the various services. That will make it easier for you to identify the big differences among the quotations. It is also common to ask for the costs of three different quantities. Not only can you see which price fits your budget, but also you will see where the price breaks occur.

Usually the mid-size or larger jobs take at least twenty-four to forty-eight hours to bid, unless of course, the printer is experiencing down time and is delighted to get it to you faster. If your job needs outside services, such as foil stamping or die-cutting, the quotes take even longer. I have worked with some printers who turn quotes around very quickly and others who seem to disappear for days before I hear from them again. If you need it fast, tell the rep. If he or she can't do it, then better luck next time.

Most quotes are valid for thirty to sixty days. However, paper prices often go up without notice. If you know for sure you will use a certain printer for the job, but not for a while, it may be worthwhile to buy the paper in advance in order to get the best price. The printer will store it for you.

When evaluating the quotes, don't look only at the price. In this age of time as a precious commodity, location can be important. If the printer is far away, and you don't have time to run back and forth for press checks, find one closer to home, even if you pay a little more. Many large companies work with printers out of state. They only go on press checks if it is absolutely necessary, and they do their communicating by means of the phone, FAX machines, and overnight delivery services.

When it comes time to make the crucial decision, consider every factor. You may be willing to pay a little more if you feel more comfortable with one of the bidders. If your favorite is much too high, ask if there may be an error in the quote. Recently, I asked a printer to look at his quote because it was so much lower than everyone else's. He called me back, thanking me over and over. It seemed his new trainee had not added in any of the prep work. If I had accepted the original quote, he would have had to honor it and eat the difference.

Insider Tips

Include a factor for ten percent over or under the quantity you ordered. Because the printer is producing a custom product, extra materials need to be ordered and printed to ensure the final count (quantity) after all the printing, finishing, and binding processes are completed.

The custom in the printing industry is to bill for the number of units actually delivered. Thus, if your order is for 4,500, you may get 4,723 or 4,958. If it's the former, that is the number on which your bill is based. If it's 4,958, however, the operative number will only be 4,950, maybe 4,500—ten percent over—and the printer will have to absorb the rest.

If all this seems too much to fuss with, simply request ten percent under and you'll get between 4,050 and 4,500.

You should also always request the cost of additional copies in the original quotation. Then you will know in advance what to expect and you'll not have to go through the bidding process again later.

Another important tidbit to know—it is the trade custom for the printer to own the negatives and plates. This helps printers get the rerun business as well. If you want to own the film or plates, negotiate up front. Remember to include that information in your contract.

Those Little Surprises

Most printers are honest folks. They want to be paid for what they do, so they include it all in the quote. Every so often I hear about one who loves to give low quotes and hit below the belt when the job is completed. The add-ons are usually legitimate charges. They simply are things that were not covered in the quote that seem to creep up. For example, most printers include at least one round of color corrections before making the plates. Rarely do you find one that makes the proof but charges later for the correction. Or a printer may quote the job on a certain paper and then switch papers to a more expensive one. I've even seen a printer mess up a blueline and try to bill the client for a new one because only one was included in the quote.

So make sure that your charges are only for what you agreed on. Be aware of the alterations or changes that you make because each one will cost you. Conversely, if you didn't ask for it, don't pay extra for it.

Printing Customs

If you are planning to purchase a fair amount of printing, it would be worthwhile to obtain a copy of the PIA (Printing Industry of America) guidelines. Although printers are not obligated to follow these trade customs (they are not legislation), many try to adhere to them. They will often rework them to suit their own business practices. You can usually find the printer's customs on the back of the quotation. Some printers will not begin a job without your signature under them.

Rather than go into full detail about the eighteen trade customs of the PIA, I suggest you ask your printer for a copy of his or her own customs. The following is merely a list of the information that the PIA customs cover:

Custom 1: Prices are valid for sixty days.

Custom 2: If you cancel an order, you must pay for the goods and services to the date (preferably in writing) of cancellation.

Custom 3: Experimental or custom work will be charged at prevailing rates and may not be used until the applicable charges are paid for.

Custom 4: All creative work done by the printer, and not expressly identified and included in the selling price, will remain as the printer's exclusive property. To use it at any point thereafter, you need to pay for the rights (unless you prenegotiated for the rights).

Custom 5: New quotations will be submitted if the original art or copy varies from the description in the original, signed quotation.

Custom 6: All preparatory materials (i.e., production artwork, film, plates) will remain the property of the printer.

Custom 7: Alterations will be charged at current rates.

Custom 8:   The printer is not liable for any errors unless you identify those errors on a *signed* pre-press proof. (Verbal instructions do not count!)

Custom 9:   Unless specifically provided in the quotation, charges for press proofs will be at the going rates. Press time lost due to customer delays or customer changes will be charged at current rates.

Custom 10:   A reasonable variation from the color proofs to the press sheets is acceptable due to a variety of production factors (i.e., differences in proofing materials, equipment, inks, paper or printing operations).

Custom 11:   Overruns or underruns will not exceed ten percent and the actual quantity delivered will be billed for.

Custom 12:   The printer will carry insurance (theft, damage, vandalism, or malicious mischief) to cover all the customer's property while it is in the printer's possession.

Custom 13:   Unless otherwise specified, the price quoted is for a single shipment, without storage. Special shipping arrangements will be billed for. Materials delivered from the customer or designated suppliers are verified with delivery tickets regarding cartons, packages, or items shown only. The printer will not be liable for the accuracy of quantities of materials based on tickets from the customer or designated suppliers. The title for the finished work will pass to the customer upon delivery or full payment, whichever comes first.

Custom 14:   Production schedules will be adhered to by the printer and the customer unless affected by actions beyond the control of either (e.g., war, floods, strikes). The final delivery date will be renegotiated if the customer does not adhere to the production schedule.

Custom 15:   Customer-furnished materials (i.e., inks, film, paper, artwork) must be manufactured, packed, and delivered to the printer's specifications. The printer can charge for specification deficiencies.

Custom 16: Payment must be made according to the terms of the quotation or invoice unless otherwise made in writing. Claims for defects, damages, or shortages must be made by the customer in writing within fifteen days or the job will be deemed acceptable.

Custom 17: The printer is liable for losing or damaging a customer's property, but liability is limited to the selling price of the damaged goods and not consequential damages, such as profit or loss. As security of payment, the printer has the right to put a lien on the goods held, including work in progress.

Custom 18: The printer is not responsible for violation of copyrights, libel, invasion of privacy, or other problems with materials provided by the customer. The customer is responsible for defending a printer being sued over the reproduction of originals or copy provided by the customer.

If you ever have any questions or doubts about the practices of a printer, the local PIA chapter will be pleased to talk to you. Of course, the ideal would be to acquaint yourself with these customs before it's too late.

CHAPTER 13

Probing the Printing Processes

Printing can be an enigmatic affair—so arcane, at times, that even some of the best designers and other creative people don't always understand it very well. Don't feel inadequate if some of the complexities of this "black art" seem somewhat tangled. Understanding printing is not unlike understanding hockey or lacrosse. You don't need to know a lot about it, but the more you know, the more you'll enjoy the game.

There are many types of printing, with different processes and applications for each. The trick is to match the job to be printed to the correct process, the one that will yield the quality needed at the price you have budgeted.

The printing processes most used by business and industry today include the following:

- Silk screen
- Flexography
- Gravure
- Photocopying
- Laser
- Ink-jet
- Digital printing
- Offset lithography

Offset lithography—offset, for short—is the process you will probably use most often, especially for projects such as brochures, annual reports, and quality product flyers. We will discuss offset printing in some depth later on.

Silk screen printing is used for short runs and for printing unusual sizes, surfaces, or shapes such as glassware, wood, plastic, metal, and fabric. Signs, T-shirts, ring boards, and sample cases are some examples of items printed by the silk-screen process.

In silk screening, ink is forced through the pores of a cloth stencil, using a squeegee. Inks can be applied more heavily than with other processes, resulting in denser and brighter colors. Silk screening is versatile; however, it is slow in both printing and drying, and it cannot reproduce photographs well.

Flexography is a high-speed method used for printing on plastics, foils, fabric, corrugated cardboard, labels, decals, and many other materials. It is especially suited to nonporous surfaces. However, grocery bags are printed flexographically because the process is very fast, and it is economical for high-volume press runs with low-grade paper.

Flexography uses rubber plates on a large press called a web. (The material to be printed on a web press comes in a roll, as opposed to sheets. Sheet-fed presses are used for most offset jobs.) Colors may be weak because the ink is thinly applied.

Gravure is used for printing high-quantity projects, such as magazines, newspaper supplements, or other jobs requiring reasonably good appearance and use of color. Ink coverage is dense, allowing a fairly high quality of reproduction even on inexpensive paper. The ideal paper for gravure is soft and smooth. Gravure is the most economical method of printing for runs ranging from 500,000 into the millions.

Photocopying transfers images electrostatically from a flat original to a belt or drum and uses heat to apply toner to the charged areas. Photocopying may be used for quantities ranging from hundreds to even thousands. For larger quantities, offset ("jiffy") printing may become more economical. This process is limited to standard sizes of 8½" × 11", 8½" × 14", or 11" × 17".

Color photocopies have improved significantly since their introduction. They are now widely available and even though cost is still high, color photocopies remain the only economically feasible way of incorporating color photographs into presentations for small audiences.

Laser printing is now common in even the smallest offices. These clever laser printers print directly from information stored in a computer. They are best used for reports, manuals, or directories.

Although images may not have the crispness and clarity as those reproduced from flat originals by a photocopier, laser printing is excellent for customized reproductions because changes in copy or art can be made easily and quickly. Laser printing is limited to legal, letter-size, or tabloid paper.

Color is an option on laser printers, but it is not very accurate, and the cost of the machines is not feasible for most businesses unless producing color work is an everyday event.

Ink-jet printers are another form of computer-driven printing. Tiny nozzles release droplets through electrostatic charging units onto the paper. The image is shaped into droplets. Ink-jet printing is quiet, fast, and dries instantly. Also, messages can be changed quickly. This method is used by mailing houses and catalog companies for addresses, personalized mailings, and direct advertisements or letters, as well as for numbering documents and tickets.

Digital printing represents an area of several emerging digital technologies which currently are geared toward the short run, pleasing (as opposed to premium) color marketplace. Digital printing is produced directly by transferring the information on the computer file to paper. This area of printing is the future of the industry. Quality and speed will be dramatically improved in the near future.

Offset lithography is the most commonly used printing process. From the ubiquitous mom 'n' pop shops—franchise or otherwise—to the huge factories that churn out billions of pages every working day, offset printers are producing most of the sea of printed materials that keep businesses afloat in the United States.

Knowing the different types of offset techniques and equipment is the only way to make cost-effective buying decisions. Quality and capabilities vary greatly—from the quick-and-dirty corner quick printer that uses paper printing plates to the supreme quality commercial house that will use state-of-the-art electronics to produce the work.

Understanding the Process

Before distinguishing among the different types of printers, it's necessary to look at how the offset process works (Figure 13.1). The basic principle of lithography is that oil and water don't mix.

The printing plate is mounted on a cylinder. The image area on the plate is water repellent, while the non-image area is water attractive. A fountain solution of water and chemicals that makes the water wetter (like when wax is on your car and the water beads) is applied to the printing plate first. The water only goes to the areas of the plate that have no image. Ink is then applied to the plate. Because the ink is oil-based and because water and oil don't mix, the ink only adheres to the image area. The balance between ink and water is a critical factor in producing quality work.

The image on the plates is transferred from the plate to a rubber "blanket" which is also mounted on a cylinder. This blanket then rotates onto the paper and prints the image. Another cylinder applies pressure under the paper to assure the complete transfer of the image.

Figure 13.1   The Offset Printing Process

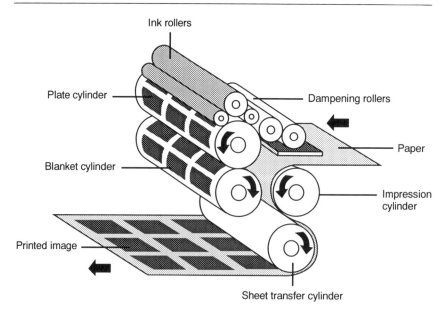

Ink rollers

Plate cylinder

Dampening rollers

Paper

Blanket cylinder

Impression cylinder

Printed image

Sheet transfer cylinder

Because the image is *offset* from the plate to the blanket before reaching the paper, the process is called *offset printing.* Because the blanket is made of rubber and is flexible, it conforms to the microscopic variations in the surface of the paper, resulting in high-quality reproductions.

When printing more than one color on a job, the process is repeated with the second (third, fourth, fifth, or sixth) color of ink at other stations, or the job is printed on a press with multi-color capabilities.

Impressive Presses

There are two types of offset presses: sheet-fed and web. The major difference is how the paper is fed into the press, which greatly affects press speed.

A sheet-fed press is precisely what it sounds like. The paper is precut into sheets. The size of the sheets varies according to the size of the press and determines how many pages can be printed at a time.

Paper that feeds into a web press comes off a large roll and is cut into sheets after printing. Web presses run at a much higher speed than sheet-fed presses, but they offer fewer choices of paper and sizes.

There are, of course, different kinds of presses within the two families. There are fairly small web presses and there are the building-size behemoths that print daily newspapers and national magazines.

Likewise, sheet-fed presses range from the little duplicators that can print paper only up to 8½" × 11", one color at a time, to the costly precision machines that can print up to eight colors at a time on sheets of paper 26" × 40" or up to 60" widths.

Just as there are differences in size, speed, and capability, there are differences in reproduction quality. The duplicator presses that are the workhorse of the quick-printing industry are capable of splendid work up to a point. The idea is to use small presses for small jobs, big presses for big jobs. There is nothing to be gained by overmatching the press to the job; it will just cost you more. But you stand to lose significantly by mismatching.

Many quick-printers advertise color printing. If they have the proper equipment, they can produce work of reasonable quality—"pleasing" color in the trade jargon. Usually, though, color printed on single-color or two-color presses is not comparable to the work that comes off presses designed specifically for color printing. The reproduction of full-color photographs and artwork is complex, intricate work and is best left to the experts.

Big Presses Are Expensive

As noted earlier, the number of inks that a press can print at once is determined by the number of cylinders through which the paper runs.

Single-color presses are the most common. They can print any color you want, but they can only do it one color at a time. Two-color presses can print two colors at once, and four-color presses—well you can guess what they do. These presses are the most common equipment.

But you will also find printers with five-, six-, and eight-color presses. (I've never head of seven-color presses and don't know why.) In addition to colored inks, the cylinders can be used to apply coatings such as varnish or aqueous laminates.

Suffice it to say, the larger the press size and the more units it has, the higher the hourly rate the press commands. The machine itself is very expensive, and the people who run it have to know more, so they get paid more.

This does not necessarily mean that a job will be more expensive if it is run on a large press. If the pages are laid out to maximize utilization of the sheet and eliminate waste, the larger presses may actually be more cost-effective because they are faster.

For example, four 11" × 17" pages can be "ganged" together on one 23" × 35" sheet. If your job is an eight-page brochure that uses the same paper stock for the cover and inside pages, the entire piece can be fitted onto one sheet and run through the press once. Ask your printer if the job will be run one-up, two-up, or any variation depending on the press size. Sometimes it is more economical to run the same pages two-up (twice) on a sheet, and other times it is best to run two different signatures (sets of pages run on a single sheet).

This is a good time to mention that you always print multiples of four pages unless the job is a single-sheet run. Take a blank 11" × 17" piece of paper and fold it in half to a size of 8½" × 11". You now have a four-page brochure (or signature). If you want an eight pager, you will print another signature and staple or stitch the two signatures together.

If you want a six-page brochure, you will have a problem. You have a choice of one more signature with two blank pages (not a good idea) or a larger sheet size (22½" × 11") folded in thirds to the 8½" × 11" size. You do not have the option of one 11" x 17" folded to four pages with a single 8½" × 11", printed both sides and inserted, if you want them bound together. Large books that are perfect bound or glued sometimes allow for insertions; nevertheless, you are still wasting the paper because sheet sizes are meant for multiples of four.

The final wrinkle in the wealth of options among presses is the perfector, a press that prints both sides of the paper at once. Some sheet-fed presses can do this, but all web presses have this capability. Indeed, some webs not only print seven colors on both sides and lay on a plastic coating all at once, but also they can cut, trim, fold, and bind each piece—all before the job comes off the press.

Printing has become an ingenious art-science-craft, and the technology continues to advance. Nonetheless it is and always will be the skill and stature of the individual printing business with which you work that will make every project a success.

A Last Word on Paper and Inks

As many years as I have been in this business, I have never been able to know enough about paper. Every time I think I finally know about all of them, a paper house discontinues one line and brings out another.

The best you can do is understand the differences and let the designer do the picking. Many of my clients show me samples of paper they like, and I have to tell them that (1) the paper does not come in a weight suitable for the job, or (2) the paper is not economical or (3) the paper has been discontinued. The following is a brief overview of the choices you can make:

Weight. Paper is measured in pounds or points (thickness). It is defined by the weight (in pounds) of a ream (500 sheets) of paper of a standard size. For example, a case of book-weight paper, 28" × 38" would weigh 50 pounds. Therefore, it would be basis 50. The paper is either a text or book weight (typically 24, 60, 70, 80, or 100 pound) or a heavier cover weight (65, 80, or 100 pound). Card stock is typically 8, 10, 12, 20, or 24 point.

The cost of the paper increases with weight or thickness. This is where the cost of a job can change dramatically. For example, you may decide to use a 100 pound book paper instead of a 65 pound cover stock. The weight is just a little different but the cost savings is significant. If you are concerned, have your designer or printer order paper *dummies* (that is, blank paper facsimiles of the size and number of pages of your project) from the paper house and compare the difference.

Finish. There are basically two finishes of paper—smooth and textured. Smooth papers include gloss, dull, or matte-coated sheets and plate finishes. Textured sheets include laid, linen, grooved, and fiber-based sheets.

Color. Stocks range in color from white to exotic colors such as plum or fuschia. If your designer suggests a colored paper, make sure the ink will read well. Just because an ink swatch looks good next to a paper does not mean it will print well. If you are really concerned, the printer can do a *draw-down* of the actual ink on the stock. This can be an expensive exercise, so get the cost up front.

As you may have noticed, more companies are using recycled papers. These papers are made by de-inking printed stock and reprocessing the paper. The "flecks" seen in many of the recycled stocks are the fibers that did not completely break down in the process. Most recycled stocks are fairly soft and porous, preventing the really crisp images of the stiffer coated stocks. As the system continues to improve, more recycled coated stocks are emerging with increasingly better quality.

All papers have aesthetic as well as practical applications. The choice of paper plays a big role in the final look and cost of the piece. A piece on newsprint, for example, will look (and actually be) less expensive than the quality look of a heavy, gloss-coated sheet.

Specifying color and inks, like specifying paper, takes training and experience. There are many different types of inks, ranging from the quick-setting inks used in offset printing to the moisture-set inks used for printing food packaging. Then there are the special metallic or fluorescent inks used for special effects. If you are requesting a special ink, ask your printer how well it adheres to the paper, if it combines well with other inks, and how difficult it is to work with. Some inks look great in the swatch book, but they cause the printers to cringe when they are specified.

Checking for the Last Time

It is not a bad idea to check all jobs as the first copies come off the press. This is the infamous press check that usually happens in the wee hours of the morning. Although, if you know and trust your printer, the press check is not something you have to worry about.

Nevertheless, it is vital to press-check jobs of four or more colors. Your designer or art director will surely be there (and will have included provision for this time in the fee). Over the years, I have made press checks at anywhere from three in the afternoon to three in the morning. But I wouldn't have it any other way.

When doing a press check on a sheet-fed press, several sheets will be pulled for you after the make-ready (press set-up) is complete and the operator feels that the color and registration are correct.

In this phase, you'll be comparing the color proofs mentioned in the chapter on pre-press production (i.e., the contact proof) to the re-production on the sheet just off the press. While you're at it, make sure the paper is correct, look for broken type, perhaps an eyelash that somehow fell onto a proof, proper registration, wrinkles, smudges, and hickeys (strange little spots of ink where they shouldn't be).

Examine the sheet for uneven ink distribution. Notice if the ink is of even *density* from page to page. You will see color bars across the top or side of the page, depending on how the sheet runs through the press. These bars are used to compare the ink density from one part of the sheet to the next and from one sheet to the next. The printer has a nifty tool, a *densitometer,* that is used to measure the amount of ink in a given area.

Also make sure the colors *trap* correctly. When two colors trap, you should not be able to see any of the color of the paper between them, nor should you be able to see their overlap with the naked eye. (However, you should see the overlap with the loop.) You can also check for *dot gain* or *dot spread.* This means that the dots are printing larger than they should and will result in a muddy image. You may even ask the operator to trim the sheets for you so you can get a preview of the real thing in proper size and shape.

Again, the professional you have hired will be doing most of this, but if there is a question only you can answer or a problem only you can solve, you need to be present during the press check.

A quality printer finds things and happily fixes them. Indeed, printers are more nitpicking about their own work than their customers are.

If you are not satisfied with something, say so. Slight adjustments can be made to color, but you must be specific about what is wrong and what you want. It is expensive to stop and start the press, and a lot of paper is wasted; therefore, be specific about your concerns.

Also, keep in mind that different papers accept inks differently. A coated, glossy paper stock will make inks look considerably different than a softer, more porous stock. Everything has limitations, so the key to a good night's sleep is to be reasonable and know what those limitations are before the job arrives at the printing plant.

In the real world, most things that companies have printed for them look great. And if the blue in the company logo isn't exactly the same as it is on your business card, you can (1) print the brochure on card stock, (2) print the card on brochure stock, or (3) don't sweat it and sign-off on the job.

Once you sign off on a sheet, you have accepted it as a sample of what all the subsequent sheets should look like. If different pages are being run on several different sheets, sign each sheet separately. Never assume that the sheet from one press run will look the same as the sheet from another run, especially if different presses are being used.

Large press runs can take hours, even days, and you will find yourself with lots of dead time or having to come back. Adjustments take time, and sometimes terrible mechanical things can happen, but it is still worthwhile to stick around and sign off on every page on every sheet. The Balderman law of fallibility states that the page you miss is the one with the problem.

Press checks are a pain, especially when a big, multicolor press with a well-paid operator and assistants are involved. But the costs are usually factored into the cost of the job.

Once you have logged some time with a quality printing house and a quality rep servicing your account, your personal involvement is not as necessary as I have stressed here. Having worked with some of the same printers for a long time, I have gained complete faith in their judgment. They know me, my work, my standards, and my clients' standards. At press-check time, I sometimes go on a "stand-by status," like an obstetrician with a patient who is ready to deliver. The rep will check the work order and whatever adjustments are indicated. When all the fiddling and fine-tuning has been done, he or she will check it again. When the work is perfect—or as close as it's going to get—*then* I'll get the call.

If it's three in the afternoon, I'll probably rush right over. If it's three in the morning, I might mumble, "If you say so, Mike. Sign off on it for me will you, old pal?"

Never One Press-Check Too Many

This brings to mind a situation that arose several years ago with one of my jobs. During the check for a very large job, something just didn't look right with the crop marks (the little lines at top, bottom, and sides showing where to trim the paper).

We were running two versions of the same four-page piece. One was to be used as an insert for a magazine and was to be printed in a 250,000 quantity on a web press. The other version was a brochure and would run in a much smaller quantity on a sheet-fed press.

To fit the magazine in which it would run, the insert had to be shorter and wider than standard brochure size. Because they were running on different kinds of presses and being printed on different paper stocks for different uses, the plates each had different line screens.

But something just didn't look right with those crop marks. Investigation revealed that the film for the plates for the magazine insert was inadvertently used for the plates on the sheet-fed press and vice-versa. This was a disaster in the making. The magazine would have rejected a quarter million four-page inserts.

Nobody had even noticed the ⅛" difference, and the client was astounded that the error was even detected. When the budget for the project was presented, this same client wondered whether it was really necessary to spend those few hundred extra dollars just to have the designer check something on the press. I would say it was worth the expenditure.

The Final Steps

The last steps before delivery happen in the bindery. After the job is printed and dry, it needs to have the finish work completed. If there is die-cutting, embossing, or foil stamping to be done, it happens at this point. Next the collating, folding, and trimming are completed. The piece is then bound together by one of many methods: perfect bound (books with individual pages are glued on the spine before the cover is attached), stapled or stitched, etc. Finally, the trimming is done.

Most smaller shops do not do their own bindery work, unless it is the type used for reports (i.e., GVC or spiral bound). Many mid-size and most large shops prefer to run their own equipment as a matter of efficiency.

At long last, the job is packaged for shipping. If you have more than one delivery location, the printer should be able to accommodate you. Of course, you probably have to pay for the extra service, especially if the deliveries are out of the area.

You may also consider printing extra quantities and having your printer store them. This saves on reprinting later. Not all printers have the space to provide this service, but it doesn't hurt to ask.

Upon delivery you will be asked to sign the delivery receipt. Now is the time to randomly check samples from different boxes. Whatever you do, don't just put them in a storeroom without checking some of the pieces. You need to catch the problems right away. I have actually signed a press proof, gone back to my office, and later discovered that in the middle of the run something happened to the plate. I would have never known if I hadn't grabbed a few random samples. If the job is being shipped elsewhere, have someone at the destination send you some samples right away.

So now you made it! Everyone is pleased, the work looks great, and because you followed all the suggestions in this book, you did it without a glitch.

So the next time the boss says, "Smithers, can you get 25,000 corporate brochures done by next week?", you can laugh and clearly explain why that is just not doable! And chances are, your clear understanding of the process and explanation of elements such as schedule, cost, or quality will dazzle others enough to believe you. If they don't, share this book with them.

CHAPTER 14

Handling Video Productions

Success and Failure of The Video Project

If your boss or whoever you report to begins by saying "Wouldn't it be nice to have a video too?," you're probably already in trouble.

Decide in advance that, for example, you're seeking a 3 percent increase in the quality of the leads you receive from a direct-mail marketing campaign by adding a video tape to the package. Then you'll have a clearly defined and measurable goal.

Now you will be able to properly design the video to achieve that objective.

In this new opportunity to serve, you'll find that most of the preliminaries are the same. You'll still have to define the problem, and you'll go about finding video production resources in much the same way you have for printed materials. The key to the success of any video project, whether it be a television commercial, a training video, a corporate sales piece, or a corporate image piece, is a clearly defined objective and a clearly defined audience.

It's really no different from any other marketing communications tool.

If you haven't decided who or how many people will view this tape, you can't possibly design a video production to achieve its objective, nor will you be able to determine what sort of budget you may have.

More realistically, you could say that there are ten thousand potential viewers across the United States that can be identified. If each of those persons would see this tape, it would be worth one dollar, two dollars, three dollars, or whatever that number might be to the company.

Once you've determined who the audience is, and what the objective is, then be certain that throughout the entire video production process, you continually review your objectives and your audience to be sure you are still on track.

The budgeting process is also pretty much the same as you read about in Chapter 5, but there are some important distinctions to keep in mind when dealing with video, as opposed to printed materials. The most important are:

Sound and motion: Video is a medium that combines sound and motion, the latter being the operative word. In video or film, the basics are the same. You have the opportunity to show things in motion: people, machines, products, services.

People can walk, talk, and demonstrate. Machines can be seen and heard in action. You can show exactly how a product or service works, and you can show the end result of what it does—the benefits.

The other side of the coin is, if the action of your people, machines, products or services is not visible, you could end up with a rather dull video.

However, camera movement can create a degree of action where little or none exists. Even so, pans, zooms in and out, and dollying can only conjure up so much action.

Simplicity: Videos do not lend themselves to being packed with intricate facts and statistics you want people to remember. A production crammed with numbers and arcane data rarely achieves the memorability its sponsors hope for.

Instead, your goal should be an overall impression of a sound, progressive business with imagination, foresight, and effective products or services.

If your viewers come away with that kind of opinion of your company, then your video has achieved its objective. If they come away numbed with numbers and delirious with facts that have been arduously and dully explained, then you've sold yourself short.

Finding and Selecting Video Producers

The process for finding good video resources is much the same as it is for finding good design resources for brochures and other printed materials. Generally video production companies specialize in entertainment, commercial or corporate and informative projects and then in specific areas, such as cars, food, high-tech or real estate projects. Check your advertising or public relations department or trade/industry associations, such as The International Television and Video Association (ITVA), The Association of Independent Commercial Producers (AICP), or The National Academy of Television, Arts and Sciences (NATAS). Even the Yellow Pages listings under Motion Picture or Video Producers can help. Also consider asking your competitors who they use or recommend.

Depending upon what part of the country you're in—how populous and how much industry is around—you may end up with a list of dozens of possibilities, or just a few. Do some preliminary telephone screening to determine each firm's experience and the kind of budgets they're used to dealing with. (The project upon which you're about to embark is known in the trade as an "industrial or corporate" video.)

Just remember, wedding videos are not the same as commercial videos. You will want to select a creative staff that has demonstrated an ability to achieve your objectives for your company. In other words, make sure that their experience level is suitable for your needs. For example, if your project is raising donations for a religious organization, you probably do not want to choose a production company whose specialty is punk-rock, "MTV" type videos.

Don't be afraid to ask for measurable results of their work. In fact, check with their clients to see if the project they produced for them achieved the results they were looking for. This should enable you to select maybe half a dozen possible resources, which you'll invite to make a presentation.

If your office has video equipment, you can ask them to come to your place to show their reels. (Actually, they are on video cassettes; *reels* is one of many trade terms carried over from the time when all productions were made on film.) In looking at these sample reels, you'll most likely see snippets of several productions. When setting your screening appointments, tell the rep that, in addition to their demo reel, you'd like to look at a complete "show" (more lingo). This will let you see how their work hangs together, a much more important factor in your decision process than looking at a series of carefully collected clips that have been artfully strung together.

After seeing their work and listening to their pitch, the good production company will have plenty of questions for you. Answer the openly and in as much detail as you can. Best of all, have a written project sheet outlining, with as much precision as possible, exactly what your project entails—and the kind of budget you have in mind.

The following is a true story and an excellent example of what *not* to do when selecting a video production company:

A novice company (one that never had purchased a video) chose to use the Yellow Pages to find companies to do their project. They selected 30 companies to provide bids on producing a corporate video. From the selected group they received 25 sample reels and proposals. The selection process became so confusing that they decided to hire a consultant to assist them in reviewing the reels and proposals. The consultant narrowed the group down to 3 finalists. The company, for no apparent reason, chose a fourth video production company to actually do the work. They paid for the video but were never able to use it because of the poor quality and objectionable content. Additional editing to resolve the problems couldn't be accomplished because the video company went bankrupt before the project was completed.

The story you have just read confirms the importance of choosing your resource wisely and adhering to a strict approval process. Furthermore, money should never change hands if you are not confident that you and your resource have the same expectations for the results, nor should you ever pay in full before a project is completed.

Setting a Video Budget

Do you know anybody who has tried to hire professionals to design and build a custom home? Surprisingly enough, there is very little difference in the process of custom home construction and producing a video. They both require a concept, a plan, materials, labor, and subcontractors; and they are produced in stages. In fact, the analogy is so close that many video production companies use the same computer accounting software programs as construction firms.

Realize that the video producer is producing a custom product for you. So the question, "What should a video cost?" is no different than, "What does a custom home cost?" It depends on the amenities or degree of sophistication of your project. You can purchase a 2,000 square foot home anywhere from $30,000 to over $1,000,000. The difference, of course, is the amenities and the location. Do you want a gravel, asphalt, or cement driveway? Do you want formica or tile counters? Do you want brass, stainless steel, or gold-plated plumbing fixtures? Quite simply, your expectations will drive the budget, so make sure you understand your choices *before* arriving at a final budget.

The cost of a custom video can range from $2,000 to over $1,000,000. Included in the options that determine the budget are:

- The number of locations required for shooting and where they are located.
- The amount of talent used and who they are. John Doe as your on-camera spokesman will cost less than Tom Cruise.
- The style and amount of animation and graphics.
- The type of music used (original or existing library stock).
- Set design and wardrobe.
- The script.
- The size of the film crew.
- The amount of editing.

A production company can give you an estimate for producing the film or video using one of two guidelines:

1. You give the production company a list of specifications you require and from that a budget is developed; or
2. You tell the production company what to spend and they create a video to fit the budget.

This, again, is similar to the custom home analogy. You begin a custom home project by meeting with an architect. He or she then develops a plan for your home (just as a writer develops a plan or script for your video). The architect can design your 2,000-square-foot home to your specifications, and the building contractor will charge you according to those specifications. Alternately, you can direct the architect to design your home to fit within your budget. Either way requires a great deal of trust in your architect. This same trust is needed in the producer of your video, so don't be afraid to tell him or her what you want!

Diagram of a Script

It is important to understand how the script drives the budget. As in the design of a custom home, your script can have as many bells and whistles as you are willing to pay for.

Figure 14.1 is a brief example of a script for a new car introduction. It is an extreme case but an excellent demonstration of what happens when you add the extras. A typical script has a scene number, the *video,* or visual description of the scene, and the *audio,* the spoken part of the scene. Since this script is for discussion purposes only, actual narrative has been cut out of the sample, except for the lead-in.

Scene 1

This first scene has four elements: the Native Americans, the horses, the car, and the location somewhere in the open plains. The footage of the Native Americans could be supplied as a stock shot available from an old Western. The car would then be dropped in at the editing phase.

On the other hand, the entire scene could be shot on location. The costs of actually shooting this scene would be very high: 1,000 extras and the crew flown to the location; plus hotels, meals, props, wardrobe, stylists and transportation; *and* prep of the car as well as the cost of finding the ideal location. The *voice-over* (VO), the voice of the narrator, would be taped in a recording studio separate from the rest of the scene.

Figure 14.1 Sample Script

Scene #	Video	Audio
1	1,000 Native Americans are seen waiting on a ridge greeting new car seen on plain below	*VO or narrator* "Years ago, when our country was an infant . . ."
2	Dissolve to animation of the continental movement during the Ice Age with car rotating on iceberg	*VO of narrator* "During the Ice Age the continents began to move . . ."
3	Cut to Charlton Heston sitting on stage with Bob Hope and Tom Cruise	*Bob Hope narration* "The three of us are selective about what we drive . . ."
4	Cut to White House with interview with President	*Mr. President* "Centuries of history stand behind the development . . ."

Scene 2

Good animation requires a great deal of skill and can be very expensive. It can also add character and interest to your video. Animation is a rendering technique, done on computer, that allows you to show an otherwise difficult visual (such as a car or a cross-section of the engine rotating upside down to right-side up). Although computers can do amazing tricks, each move must be rendered separately by a trained computer artist. The levels of the quality of animation can vary greatly and become quite obvious when viewed on the completed video. If your budget does not allow for the best quality animation, either simplify the

Figure 14.1a   Sample Video Board

rendering, use stock images (if possible), or eliminate it completely. In this scene, it would be possible to merge stock animation of ice-breakers with custom animation of the car rotating in order to cut the expenses a bit. The narration of this scene would be done at the same time as that of scene 1.

Scene 3

Hiring top-name talent can drive the best budget out of the ball park. This scene not only requires expensive talent, but another location shot. This means more costs for set-up and wrap, stage rental, transportation of the crew and equipment, wardrobe and stylists. If the footage of these three actors together on stage actually already existed, it would still be expensive to use because of royalty fees and the time it would take to research the existence of the shot. In addition, Bob Hope would still demand a handsome fee for the narration on camera. If budget is a concern, this would be a scene to eliminate.

Scene 4

Hiring the President of the United States to endorse or promote your product is a bit unlikely. But if you could, imagine the expenses. In addition to the usual production and travel costs, you would most likely have to pay for the time and expenses of the staff he brings along, from assistants to security. Stock footage of the President may be available. Consider showing the footage but substituting the voice-over of an actor talking about the importance of a strong leader (alluding to the car) rather than the voice-over of the President. Sometimes there are other, less expensive ways to make the same statement.

Requesting a Proposal

You are ready to send a request for proposal (RFP) to your selected video production companies once you have decided if you will be providing a budget or specifications. Whatever you do, *do not* provide both and *do* give the same information to all of the companies.

The sample RFP (Figure 14.2) gives a lot of information about the content and desired length of the video as well as a budget range. Notice that it also includes a situation analysis, who the target audience is, what the objectives and strategies are and the specific requirements for the schedule.

In their proposal, the video production company must define their creative approach and provide a detailed budget breakdown to show how and where the dollars will be spent. Another option is to submit a creative approach or script with the list of specifications in the RFP. However, if you do not understand the video production process, it is best to leave the creative to the professionals.

The Production Cost Estimate

Figure 14.3 shows a typical production cost summary that should be submitted to all of the companies bidding the video project so that you can later analyze their bids on an equal basis. The breakdown includes all of the elements:

- The personnel involved and how long they will be needed.
- The location expenses and travel (where applicable).
- The props and wardrobe.
- Studio rentals and expenses.
- Set design and construction.
- Equipment usage (cameras, audio, grip, lighting, cranes and helicopters).
- Raw stock (film or tape).
- Processing and transfer.
- Director and creative fees (including research, writing and directing).
- Talent.
- Talent expenses.
- Post production (including packaging, duplication, assembly and shipping).

Figure 14.2   Request for Video Proposal

From: _____

Contact: _____

Address: _____

Phone: _____ FAX: _____

Date: _____

Situation Analysis:

_____

_____

_____

_____

_____

Assignment:

_____

_____

_____

_____

_____

Target Audience:

_____

Objectives:

_____

_____

_____

Strategies:

_____

_____

_____

_____

Rationale:

_____

_____

_____

_____

Figure 14.2   Request for Video Proposal *(continued)*

Bid/Budget:

To include all of the following:

_____

_____

_____

_____

_____

_____

_____

_____

Do not include the following:

_____

Budget:

The budget on this bid will be *fixed (or open-ended).*

It may not exceed $ _____

Schedule:

Request for proposal	_____
Bids from production company	_____
Award job	_____
Script to client	_____
Final script	_____
Pre-production	_____
Begin production	_____
Edit/Dupe	_____
Client review	_____
Final edit/Dupe	_____
Dupe/Collate	_____
Delivery (Ship 3 day)	_____

Figure 14.3 Film and Video Production Estimate

Agency: _____   Production company: _____

Name: _____   Name: _____

Address: _____   Address: _____

City, State, Zip: _____   City, State, Zip: _____

_____   _____

Phone: _____   Phone: _____

Fax: _____   Fax: _____

Client: _____   Producer: _____

Title: _____   Writer: _____

Agency contact: _____   Director: _____

Client contact: _____   Editor: _____

Bid date: _____   File name: _____

Summary of estimated costs

Pre-production and wrap costs	Total A&C	
Shooting crew labor	Total B	
Location and Travel expense	Total D	
Props and Wardrobe	Total E	
Studio expenses	Total F	
Set Construction	Total G&H	
Equipment costs	Total I	
Raw Stock, Develop and Transfer	Total J	
Miscellaneous	Total K	
Sub-Total A–K		
Director/Creative fees	Total L	
Sub-Total Direct Costs		
Production Fee		
Talent	Total M&N	
Post Production	Total O	

Total Estimate	

Figure 14.3   Film and Video Production Estimate *(continued)*

Crew:	A: Pre-pro/Wrap				B: Pre-light/shoot				
	Days	Rate	O.T.	Total	No.	Days	Rate	O.T.	Total
Executive Producer									
Producer									
Coordinator									
Assistant Director									
Cinematographer									
Video Engineer									
Art Director									
Prop Master									
Gaffer									
Best Boy									
Electrician									
Electrician									
Key Grip									
Best Boy									
Grip									
Grip									
Audio Mixer									
Boom Operator									
Make Up									
Hair									
Wardrobe									
Script Clerk									
Home Economist									
Video Assist Oper									
Special Effects									
Teleprompter									
Location Scout									
Production Asst.									
Craft Service									
Helicopter Pilot									
Aerial Cameraman									
Policemen									
Fireman									
Medical Tech.									
Teacher/Welfare									

Sub-Total A		Sub-Total B	
PT/P&W		PT/P&W	
Total A		Total B	

(continued)

Figure 14.3   Film and Video Production Estimate *(continued)*

C: Pre-production and wrap costs	No.	Days	Rate	Total
Auto Rentals				
Air fares				
Per-Diem				
Still Camera, film & processing				
Deliveries				
Trucking				
Casting director				
Casting facilities				
Working meals				
			Total C	

D: Location Expenses	No.	Days	Rate	Total
Location fees				
Permits				
Tracking				
Mileage				
Motorhome				
Car prep. & Transport				
Vehicle rental				
Airfare				
Airfreight				
Hotels				
Per-Diem				
Craft Service				
Meals				
Security guards				
			Total D	

E: Props, Wardrobe & Animals	No.	Rate	Total
Prop purchase/rental			
Wardrobe purchase/rental			
Picture Vehicles			
Animals & Handlers			
		Total E	

Figure 14.3   Film and Video Production Estimate *(continued)*

F: Studio Rental and Expense	No.	Days	Rate	Total
Build days				
Pre-light days				
Shoot days				
Wrap days				
Stage manager				
Power/Generator				
Phones, coffee, etc.				
Craft service				
Meals				
			Total F	

G: Set Construction	No.	Rate	Total
Set Designer			
Set Construction crew			
Tracking			
Mileage			
Set Wrap			
		Total G	

H: Set Construction Materials	No.	Rate	Total
Set purchase			
Materials			
Set Rentals			
Trucking & Mileage			
Special Effects			
Prop rental			
Prop Purchase			
		Total H	

(continued)

Figure 14.3   Film and Video Production Estimate *(continued)*

I: Equipment Rental	No.	Days	Rate	Total
Camera Equipment				
Special Lenses				
Audio Equipment				
Grip truck and equipment				
Mileage				
Lighting equipment				
Generator & delivery				
Camera car				
Dolly/Crane				
Car Mounts				
Video assist/Monitors				
Helicopter				
Teleprompter				
Walkie Talkies				
Supplies and Expendables				
			Total I	

J: Raw Stock, Develop, Transfer	No.	Rate	Total
Film stock			
Film Processing			
Audio tape			
Audio transfers			
Video Tape			
Film to tape transfers			
Stock for video transfer			
Off-line copies			
Transfer supervision			
		Total J	

K: Miscellaneous	No.	Rate	Total
Petty cash			
Phones/Faxes			
Shipping			
Deliveries			
Insurance			
		Total K	

Figure 14.3   Film and Video Production Estimate *(continued)*

L: Director/Creative fees	No.	Days	Rate	Total
Research				
Writing				
Storyboards				
Director's Prep Days				
Director's Travel Days				
Director's Shoot Days				
Director's Post Days				

	Sub-Total L	
	PT/P&W	
	Total L	

M: Talent	No.	Days	Rate	OT/Travel	Total
Principal talent					
Principal talent					
Narrators					
Extras					
Extras					
Stuntmen					
Precision drivers					
Hand models					

	Sub-Total M	
	PT/P&W	
	Handling Fee	
	Total M	

N: Talent Expenses	No.	Days	Rate	Total
Travel: Mileage, airfare, etc.				
Hotel, Per-Diem				
Wardrobe Allowance				

	Sub-Total N	
	Handling Fee	
	Total N	

(continued)

Figure 14.3 Film and Video Production Estimate *(continued)*

O: Post-Production	No.	Rate	Total
Graphics			
Animation			
Music			
Narration recording			
Sound Effects			
Audio transfers			
Audio lay-down/lay-back			
Audio sweetening			
Digitizing			
Off-line			
Lay off — dubs & delivery			
Re-digitizing			
2nd Cut off-line			
Lay-off dubs & delivery			
On-line			
ADO			
Chyron			
Matte Camera			
Sub-Masters			
Edit Master			
Protection Master			
Duplication Master			
Dubs & delivery			
Mass Duplication			
Labels			
Packaging			
Assembly			
Shipping			
Delivery Service (FedEx, UPS, etc.)			
	Sub-Total O		
	Handling Fee		
		Total O	

The next chapter will go into detail about the actual production of a video. But first take some time to understand the elements and people involved. It is important to know that there are many books written on the subject of producing videos. Since your goal should be to understand enough to read a proposal and agree to the costs involved, this book will only cover the basics.

Figure 14.4 is a typical illustration of a timeline and payment schedule for the tasks involved in producing a corporate video. Once you have reviewed it, the production cost summary will be easier to follow. Keep in mind that video production can be as elaborate and time consuming as the budget and schedule permit. You can help meet deadlines and the budget with quick review and approvals. In addition, it is less expensive to make changes at the script development stage than the production stages.

The following is a breakdown of the production cost estimate. It includes every possible expense that could be encountered, however, not all videos require every item listed.

Pre-Production, Wrap-Up, and Shooting Crew Labor

Pre-production and wrap-up expenses include all of the fees to set-up and wrap-up a shoot, while the shooting crew labor fees cover the costs of hiring the labor needed to actually shoot the video. These costs will cover every member of the crew involved in the shoot, including: the *producer, director,* the *cameramen,* the *art director, prop master, gaffer, key grip* and all of their assistants, the *audio mixer, boom operators, make-up* and *hair stylists, wardrobe assistant, script clerk,* a *home economist* and the *video assist operator.* All of these terms are described in the glossary of this book. Your video may even require the presence of a fireman if there is a potential fire hazard, a police officer if the city requires one to be on location to direct traffic or on-lookers away from the shoot, a medical technician for emergencies or a teacher/welfare worker if there is a child on the set under 18 years of age. Child labor laws require one teacher/welfare worker for every 10 children under 18.

Part of the expense of pre-production includes the cost of a *location scout* to find locations for shooting. You will pay for the scout's car to

Figure 14.4   Timeline and Payment Schedule for Producing a Video

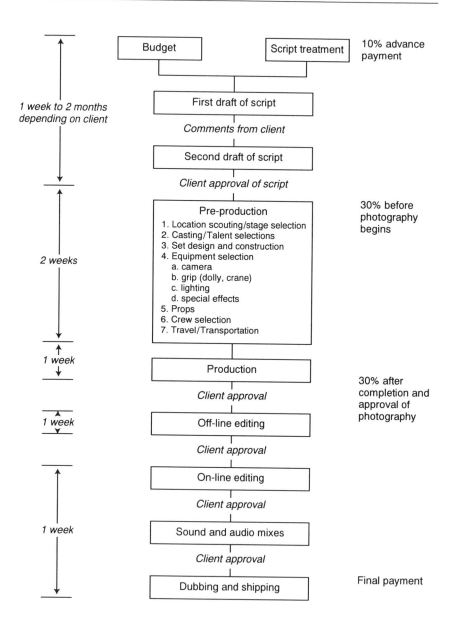

drive to different potential sites, as well as air fare and per diem for out-of-town travel. You will also pay for still shots of the various potential locations. During this phase you will also have the costs of the *casting director* to go to the various talent agents in order to select the talent to appear at the *casting call*. Another charge is for the *casting facility,* a location used to review the abilities of the talent and select the ones for your video. You will even see a charge for all of the meals eaten by the staff and talent during this phase.

Location Expenses

Location fees can range greatly, depending on the location. Different sites have different usage fees as well as permits from the city where you are shooting. A variety of vehicles, including trucks for transporting gear, props and sets, buses for transporting the talent and crew, motorhomes and *honey wagons,* must be used on location, used for crew and talent to change clothes and for restroom facilities.

If you are shooting cars, there will be a fee for the preparation of the vehicles as well as getting them to the location. Other transportation costs may include auto rentals, airfare or air freight if you need to move a lot of large equipment. Then, of course, you will have the cost for the crew and talent's hotel, meals and *craft service* (snacks and refreshments). If equipment is left at the location overnight there will be a fee for a security guard.

Props, Wardrobe, and Animals

Parts of the sets (for example: trees, furniture, dishes, computers, etc.) usually are rented props. There will be a fee for every prop used. Additionally, the wardrobe for the talent, whether purchased or rented, will be included as a cost. Occasionally animals are used in videos. These animals usually come with handlers. There are strict laws about how animals can be used in films or videos and the handler knows how to make the animal perform, and what they are allowed to do. If you are using an animal, you will pay for the animal and the handler.

Studio Expenses

If you will be shooting in a studio, there will be a fee for studio rental and the studio manager for each day you will use the studio. Additional fees will include the use of stages and the time for setting up (*building*) the set, setting-up the lighting and the set tear down (*wrapping*) the set. There will also be a fee for the power used to run all of the equipment as well as a fee for the craft service and meals for the crew.

Set Construction and Materials

Every aspect of building a set will be included as a cost, from design to construction and delivery. Every nail, can of paint and the time for the crew to buy the materials will be included. Occasionally, sets are rented rather than built. Either way, a fee will be included for transporting the sets to the stage once they are built or assembled and then wrapping them and removing them. You may also see a prop rental charge in this category.

Equipment Rental

There will be a fee for every piece of equipment used in producing a video. You will recognize some, such as cameras, lenses, walkie talkies, lights or the teleprompter. Others may be unfamiliar. You will see words like *grip, dolly and video assist*. These terms apply to equipment commonly used in the trade. Unless you hope to go into the video biz, it isn't necessary to know what each item does (however they are defined in the glossary in the back of this book), just be aware that they exist so that you recognize them as a necessary cost. Some shots require the use of helicopters. This may be expensive, but sometimes necessary to get the shots you want.

Raw Stock

Raw stock is film and video and audio tape. Once the film or video is shot and the audio recorded, it will be developed, then edited, and transferred to a final copy. All of the cost for time and materials involved will be included.

Miscellaneous

Little costs can add up to big ones, especially if a lot of the work is done on location. Every one of these "little" charges, such as phone/fax, shipping, deliveries, couriers or petty cash will be itemized as a cost. An important cost, sometimes overlooked by the client, is insurance. Equipment needs to be insured. Many locations require indemnification policies. There is also liability for injury and other types of required protection. In fact, you may need as many as two dozen different policies. If you are at all concerned about who is responsible for what, where, when and how, discuss this up-front with your production company. They are very aware of the importance of insurance and would be foolish not to include it. For an additional fee you can get duplicates of each policy required.

Director and Creative Fees

In order to write a script, the writer must do research, for which there is a research fee. Then there will be a set fee for writing the actual script. In addition there are storyboards. These are sketches of the key frames of the video to give the client an idea of what will be produced.

Be prepared to pay for every aspect of the director's involvement. First, he will have prep days that include meeting with the art director, the writer, the producer and the client to demonstrate his understanding of the project and what it should look like. He will then have travel days and, of course, shoot days. He will also be involved in part of the post-production to ensure that his visions are properly transferred to the final medium.

Additional Expenses

Production Fees

Generally you will find a production fee in addition to the expenses listed above. This fee covers overhead and a risk factor (the same as the "contingency fee" that was discussed earlier in this book in reference to print creative and production estimates). Generally, the risk factor increases proportionally with the complexity of the project. This fee covers unforeseen expenses. Typically, production fees run anywhere from 15 to 45 percent of the direct expenses totaled on lines A through L on the production cost summary.

Talent

Talent fees include time plus add-on expenses including union, pension, welfare, payroll taxes, and miscellaneous expenses such as travel and wardrobe—and a handling fee. Talent may also include stuntmen, precision drivers (for scenes with cars), or hand models. Sometimes the numbers seem excessive, but without good talent there is no reason to continue the project.

Post-Production

Generally post-production is included as a separate element, including its mark-up and expenses. Post-production includes all of the work required to complete the video once the shooting is finished, such as: graphics (title backgrounds and logos), animation (for animating difficult to shoot visuals), narration recording, original or library music, sound effects, *audio lay-down* and *lay-back, sweetening* and transferring, off-line and on-line editing, tape production and transfer, dubs, duplication, packaging and shipping. (These terms are explained in the glossary of this book.

A video of the magnitude outlined in the sample production cost summary is one of first quality. In fact, it could be compared to the type of production necessary for a television show. You may not need everything listed, but it is always best to be aware of all of the possibilities. With a detailed cost estimate in hand and final discussions of goals and objections detailed for your production company, you are ready to go into production.

CHAPTER 15

Producing the Video:
From Script to Finished Product

The Almighty Script

Film and video, it is often said, is the director's medium. But without a proper script, even Speilberg or Coppola couldn't direct a good production for you. Most production houses have a stable of writers they work with regularly. Ask about them. And pay attention to the writing in the sample show you watch.

You don't necessarily have to use a production house's writer. You can hire your own if you don't care for what they have to offer. An advantage of hiring an independent writer is that you will not be locked into a production house at this stage. It can be to your advantage to interview two or three production finalists, then have them submit bids based on the detailed treatment (see below) your writer will come up with.

If you are working on other marketing materials at the same time, ask your agency or writers if they also write scripts. Many of the good ones do. You'll certainly end up with a more cohesive program if all of the pieces have the same flavor.

In this medium, you must measure writing not just by its clarity and crispness, but also by the ability of the narrator or spokespersons to handle it. If there's a lot of mush mouth, awkward structures and difficult word series—a bunch of "s" sounds strung sinuously together, there is a problem. Writing to be read and writing to be spoken are two different things.

Keep those sample tapes from the production companies for a while. Watch them several times, then listen to them. Do the words flow? Are they easy for the narrator to say? Do they have color and rhythm? Are they lively and to the point? Are they interesting? And do they get the job done?

Remember the analogy of the custom house to the video production? A good writer or video producer will know how to write a script that matches your objectives, strategies, and budget. Since the production costs will reflect what is necessary to produce the script, make sure that your expectations are clear to the writer. If you give him or her full rein to be creative, don't expect the result to match a tight budget.

Before the Script There Was . . .

Every video production takes scripting in three stages.

The first is the *Concept Statement*. This comes out of "think sessions," where windows are stared out of, crumpled bits of paper are tossed into wastebaskets, and ideas are kicked around and percolated.

The concept statement is simply a paragraph or two or four which describe the idea. How the show opens, where it goes and how it ends. We usually come up with four to six of these, walk away for a couple of days, and then come back with some objectivity. Often, what was once a great, great, great idea suddenly isn't. Or, if we're lucky, that idea gets more "greats."

We settle on two of these and then present them to our client. We never present an idea that we wouldn't want to see produced—no throwaways. But we also always have a recommendation and reasons why.

Once we've agreed on the concept, we then do stage 2: write a *Treatment*. This is a detailed outline, describing all the important scenes and briefs of what the narration and/or on-camera talent will be saying. Less important scenes are listed, and any production details noted.

This gives the client an overall view of what the production will be like, what it will cover and with what emphasis, what kind of talent will be used and how the show will flow from scene-to-scene. A good treatment also gives the production house an accurate guide for coming up with a firm budget. At this point, there should be no surprises.

The treatment stage is when all the details should be discussed. Client and writer should agree on every detail: Add more emphasis here, decrease there. Agree on whether there will be an on-camera spokes-person or a "voice-over" narrator, what is shot on location, what is shot on a sound stage and so on through the entire production.

You, as the client, either approve the treatment as written or as revised. If you need approvals from up the corporate ladder, now is the time to get them. Once the approval-in-principle cycle is complete, give your writer the go-ahead for the final stage, to write *The Script* and have the two or three production houses you have selected prepare bids based on the approved treatment.

The only significant difference that may arise is that, in writing the final script, the writer may come up with even better ideas. Sometimes these will affect the budget, so be sure to give the production houses preparing bids the opportunity to review the script and make any budget adjustments that may be necessary. If these result in an increased budget, then you'll have to decide whether the new ideas are worth the added expense.

Pre-Production Planning

If you receive bids that don't cover this vital category, get very suspicious. Proper detailed pre-production planning can save you a ton of money—and help ensure that the right video comes out the other end.

Pre-production involves meetings and planning of all of the key players, such as the director, the writer, the producer and you, the client. It also includes casting, location scouting, scheduling, planning out all of the equipment, crew and talent usage, transportation, meals and hotels and more details than you can imagine. This isn't the place to question a line-item charge of a few hundred, or even a few thousand, dollars.

This is the place to make sure you get everything figured out—not when there's a stage full of talent and crew.

What Format?

If you are producing an industrial film, you only have four choices: 8, 16, 35, or 70 millimeter. If there is to be some animation of footage downstream, you will probably choose 35mm.

In video, it gets more complex. The tried-and-true medium for industrials has been ¾-inch, U-Matic video. But technical developments in recent years are consigning ¾-inch to the dinosaur exhibit. Even so, you can still get respectable results under normal lighting conditions. The medium of choice for the past several years has been Sony's ½-inch Betacam. Even more recently, many industrials are being taped on Sony's Hi 8 equipment with fine results.

While your old camcorder uses ½-inch tape, it is not even close to the quality of professional ½-inch. Nor is the 8mm format anything like the Super 8 film of yore.

Casting

Casting is an important aspect of any production. Imagine for a moment Ethel Merman or Bobcat Goldthwait cast as narrators for a relaxation tape. The rule of thumb here is to require that individuals perform the tasks you will ask them to do in the production.

Normally the production company's *casting director* will handle the procurement of all talent. You should certainly be given the opportunity to approve his or her final choices, but leave the screening process and finalist selections to this experienced person.

If you will need a narrator, the casting director will ask the prospective talent to read from the script. He will make an audiotape of the reading and use it in the selection process. For straight narration—called a *voice-over* or, as indicated in the script, *vo*—he will not necessarily need to meet the talent in person, nor will you. An audiocassette of the prospective narrator reading your copy will suffice because the quality of the voice and the intelligence behind the reading will come through on the tape.

If you will need on-camera actors, the casting director will do a first *casting call*. For a corporate video, the talent agents will send 40 or 50 prospective actors who fit the description of the character for each role. They will all appear on a given date at the *casting facility* to do a first audition. At this audition the casting director has an opportunity to view the talent live and, if their role will be spoken, to have them read a page from the script. The production house will make videotapes of the auditions of the on-camera talent. Some actors change drastically in front of the camera—and not always for the better. It is not necessary for the client to appear at the first audition, nor is it always your best use of time.

From the preliminary audition, 5 or 6 prospective actors are selected for each role for a *call back*. They then come to a second audition at the casting facility. Usually the director joins the casting director at this audition. Although it is not necessary, you may choose to be there also. The director and casting director will sort out the chaff and present you with the finalists. Undoubtedly you will have some favorites among the selection. (If you don't, have your casting director go back to the talent agents and start again.)

Some years ago, we produced a spot in which the devil himself starred. We auditioned more than a dozen actors, but the client would not pay the few hundred dollars extra for taping. At the audition, there was no question about who should get the part. The client loved this one fellow who was a wonderful devil—menacing, but with a nice, soft edge.

He was not our first choice, but since the client is almost always right, we agreed.

At the shoot, the devil turned into a wimp. Had we taped him, this would have been evident, but we were so engrossed with his delivery, we didn't notice his wimp-limp mannerisms.

To save a few hundred bucks, a whole shoot day went down the drain.

Get it on tape, then decide!

Film or Tape

Nearly all network-quality commercials are shot on film. The film is then transferred to videotape. Most corporate productions are shot on video-tape and similarly edited electronically.

The real difference between film and videotape for original pho-tography is subjective and very subtle. Film has an indefinable, mystical look, where video has a more realistic look. Can you imagine the movie *On Golden Pond* having the real look of *News at 7?* Conversely, the series *COPS* or the *News at 7* would seem fake or contrived with images and visuals shot on film like *On Golden Pond.*

Each media has its own advantages and applications. Any profes-sional production house should have the experience and flexibility to recommend shooting on film or tape, according to which will deliver the desired visual effect and achieve the stated objective.

Once you've decided whether you are going to create your original photography on film or on videotape, you'll select which format you will use within that medium. On film, your choices are basically 16mm, 35mm, or if you're very extravagant, 70mm. Generally, the larger the film format, the greater the resolution or sharpness of the image captured on film and, also, the greater the sharpness of the final image.

Again, consider watching the movie *On Golden Pond,* which was released on 70mm. Even after being transferred to video for your home VHS player, the quality is still superb. There is some justification for larger format in any situation, but budget may prohibit the extravagance of 70mm. Certainly 16mm is more than acceptable for many regional television commercials and most corporate productions.

On video it becomes more complex, Today the advances in video cameras, recorders and tape stock in recent years have converted many former film-only fanatics.

In the "old days," video people used to pump in as much light as they could find—just blast the set with it—which gave a flat, mechanical feel to the pictures. But now, videographers and their lighting directors can "paint" a scene with light every bit as dramatically as their film counterparts. Indeed, many camera people today will work with video one day, film the next—and defy most people to tell the difference.

In some ways, video is easier and safer, because of WYSIWYG—"What You See Is What You Get"—on the monitor. But today, film producers combine the best of both worlds by using "video assist," a video camera synchronized with the film camera and showing what's being photographed on a monitor.

Any professional production house should have the experience and flexibility to recommend shooting on film or tape, according to which will deliver the desired visual affect and achieve the stated objective.

A major factor that might swing the production medium to film is how you will use the end result. For example, it is usually better to project onto a screen when showing to a large viewing audience. This, of course, would result in a choice of film.

It costs a lot less to rent a 16mm projector than it does a gaggle of huge projection TV sets. As far as production costs, the bottom lines are usually quite similar.

The Shoot

This is really the easy part. All the decisions have been agonized over and made. The script is perfect. Everything is marvelous.

Shooting will either occur on a stage or on location. A stage is a set in a production studio. Location shooting can include anything from sending a crew to your local office to shoot footage of the production facility to reenacting the Ten Commandments in Israel. Obviously, the more complex the shoot, the more crew members and talent you will see on the set.

If you are shooting on location, you may see all kinds of vehicles: trucks to transport equipment, props or sets, "honey wagons" to be used for changing clothes and as restroom facilities, motor homes for the crew to sleep in, and cars.

The crew members will build the sets and set up the lighting, cameras, audio equipment, electrical equipment, props and wardrobe and prepare the actors to appear in their roles. So, sit back in the director's chair the production house will surely have for you, and enjoy. Watch these fine craftsmen at work—smooth, efficient, capable.

If you believe something is being done incorrectly, have a quiet little chat with the producer, then let him call the director aside and the three of you can hash it out. If you feel an actor is delivering his or her lines incorrectly, or the lighting is too dim, or whatever . . . *please,* let the director handle it. On a set—even on location in your own plant or office—there can be only one boss and that is the director.

Yes, some directors are a little top-heavy in the ego department. But there's a tested method of resolving on-set disputes. Have the director shoot something two ways: your way and his. The director is responsible for translating your script into an effective visual presentation. Cut him or her some slack. You are responsible for the whole thing coming out right. So make sure he'll cut you some, too.

There are also times when things happen: sometimes bad things, sometimes great things. An actor or spokesperson will accidentally fluff a line. And maybe it works better than what the script called for. Or maybe the cameraman will look through the lens and see something nobody had expected. If you're lucky, there can be a major improvement in that scene.

If you're unlucky, then you may have to rethink a lot of things. We once contracted to produce a demonstration film for a company in Reno that had revolutionized road scraping. They had come up with this device that operated on harmonics, rather than mechanical effort. The trouble was that when we showed up on the location site at daybreak, the machine wouldn't work. Nothing its inventor did could get it to work.

The five of us packed up all the gear and flew back to Los Angeles with hardly a foot of usable film in the can.

We consoled the company president with the thought that, "Hey, it could be worse. Suppose you had a whole squad of executives from John Deere or Caterpillar out here (companies they were soliciting for funding) and *then* it didn't work?"

And therein lies the beauty of a product demonstration video: Everything comes off in only the best light. P.S. We went back the next week for two days and made a wonderful—if slightly over budget—film.

Once the filming is over, you and the talent can head home, but the production crew has to stay behind in wrap up the set. Everything needs to be taken down and transported back to where it came from, whether it was from a rental house or the production company's storage facility.

Post-Production

All the planning, revising, recording, and shooting come together in post-production. At this stage, the pictures, the sound, and the narration become one.

We will assume that your production has been shot in Betacam format. The original footage has been transferred to ¾-inch tape for *off-line editing* and 1-inch for *on-line editing.* First, your production is edited off-line to make a *rough cut,* which you will review and change if necessary. After your approval, the tape is revised and refined during the process of on-line editing to make the final version.

Let's backtrack to the off-line editor who is a very important person in the success of your video. During off-line editing, the editor sits down with the script and all the footage. He or she then assembles the footage in sequence. Some editors prefer to work in chunks, assembling the shots in scenes. Others start from the beginning and assemble the scenes in consecutive order.

The off-line editor's work is analogous to the production person who assembles the type, artwork, and other elements of the page on computer or on art boards. The difference, however, is in the technology involved.

During the shoot, the director has decreed which takes will be *circled.* These takes are the "keepers"; the rest end up on the often mentioned cutting room floor. The editor then links the selected takes together electronically, using a set of working tapes in one recorder as the source. Slowly, scene by scene and take by scene, the mass of videotape begins to take shape.

The editor is in charge of handling various techniques that don't show up in the rough footage. Among these techniques are *cuts* and *dissolves.*

A cut is an abrupt scene change. For example, when you watch an interview, you'll notice that footage of the interviewer is used when a question is asked. The scene then cuts abruptly to the interviewee for the answer. During the answer, the footage may cut to a close-up of the person's hands and then cut back to a medium shot of the person's face. Each change or cut in the scene is the work of the editor.

The other technique, called dissolve, involves the effect of one scene overlapping the following scene. This effect is also created by the editor.

The purpose of the editor's work, in addition to assembling the countless elements of the production, is to create the drive, pace, and rhythm that are appropriate for your project. The right drive, pace, and rhythm enhance the production; the wrong ones drag it down.

During off-line editing, the recorded voice-over is added, and sometimes music is added where needed. (For many projects, music is obtained from music libraries that license their work for modest fees.) Throughout the process, the editor painstakingly runs the tape back and forth many times, trimming a little here or adding a little there.

Off-line editing may take from a few hours to a few days, depending on the length and complexity of your production. In general, we estimate that an off-line editor can do four cuts or dissolves an hour.

Finally, it's time: The "rough cut" is ready for you to see. In most cases, you'll have to use your imagination a bit. The sound is not yet equalized, some effects and music are missing, and dissolves and other visual effects usually have not been added. (Cuts are abrupt scene changes; dissolves are where you see a little of the old scene overlaps the upcoming scene. See the glossary.)

Rough-cut stage is when you make changes. If you do it during the "on-line" edit session, it will cost you a ton of dough.

If the rough cut is according to script and you still want to make changes—for example, you don't like the narration in a particular spot—it's relatively simple and inexpensive to do so. (Although if the show is according to script and you do make changes, you are obligated to pay any charges for doing so.

Once your client has approved the off-line version of your video production, the next step is the on-line edit. On-line editing is nothing more than confirming the camera originals, whether film or tape, to the off-line edit. Again, with the analogy to printing, this is the printer's press time versus the layout time.

The well-prepared editor will come to the on-line session with a carefully detailed "edit list." These days, most off-line editing systems can generate a tape or disk that drives the on-line.

In on-line, you are laying down, take-by-take, from the master tape. This is done by time-coded numbers on the work tape, which corresponds to those on the master.

The assembly is then being recorded on an "edited master" tape, usually in 1-inch format, Beta cam, or, more recently, a digital format such as D1 or D2.

If your script calls for dissolves and other visual effects, they are put in here. If you want your company's new widget to spin onto the screen, or come up from infinity to full screen, that's done here. For spinning things and similar tricks, the on-line editor calls into play a device that can make just about anything move any way you want it to.

We had an on-line session once where the client mused aloud how nice it would be if his products could pop-on the screen in little boxes. He had seen something like that in a commercial the night before. We suggested that the commercial he had seen probably had an on-line budget greater than his entire show, but he was sold on the idea. It cost him an extra $4,000. And then he didn't like it.

PAL No Longer Means Friend

The on-line is over, you're on time and on budget. Drinks all around! But before, make sure the edit studio takes your final edited master and immediately makes two more masters from that.

First the edit studio will make a *protection master*. This master, a duplicate of the original, is stored separately as a back-up. The *dubbing master* is what you'll use for producing the quantity of copies you have specified. These copies will probably be made in VHS format, but you may also want ¾-inch copies.

There are three basic formats in use throughout the world: NTSC in the United States; PAL in most of the other English-speaking countries, Japan and other parts of Asia; and SESAM in France and Russia. It isn't important that you know the technical differences among these formats, nor do you need to know what the alphabet soup stands for.

Any *dub house* (the place where duplicate tapes are made) should be able to exactly match your format requirements to the countries for which you need copies. As soon as the copies are made, labeled, packaged, shipped and delivered, your job is done. You have successfully managed a video production. Congratulations!

CHAPTER 16

Putting It All Together

Now that you have learned the steps it will take to help you design cost-effective and successful marketing tools, it's time to put them to use. This chapter will give you an opportunity to see the forms in this book applied to a typical marketing program. And the best part is that you can break the entire process down into four simple steps. Just follow them, and you will be on your way to easy street.

In order to set the stage, let's develop a hypothetical scenario for developing a marketing campaign for a soon-to-be-released product for industrial use. Let's assume that you have already worked through Checklists 1 and 2 and determined what tools you will use in your marketing campaign. You are the product manager, Susan Jones. It will be your responsibility to oversee the entire project and report directly to the president of the company, Bill Big. The campaign will include one full-page, four-color ad, an eight-page, four-color brochure with photographs, and an eight- to ten-minute video. You will shoot the video and photographs in two locations. You have decided that you want to find a small advertising agency to handle everything, including the video. Although it is more desirable to have the same photographer and video crew for everything, the advertising agency and video company will use local crew, equipment and talent for each location to avoid excessive travel costs.

For the sake of efficiency (and review), let's work through the complete process of developing these tools step-by-step. After that, you will be ready to be on your own:

Step 1—Establish an Erg List

Unit of Work (Erg)	Who Does It?	How Long?
Define problem	Susan	1 day
Establish budget	Bill Big & Susan	2 days
Brief internal staff	Susan	1 day
Redefine problem	V.P. Marketing (Ed S.) and Susan	2 days
Interview agencies	Susan & Ed	1 week
Discuss redefined problem	Ed & Susan	1 day
Review & approve redefined budget	John	1 day
Secure preliminary bids from agencies	Susan	4 days
Select agency	Ed & Susan	1 day
Gather information for agency	Susan	1 month
Develop preliminary schedule	Susan	1 day
Gather preliminary information	Susan	5 days
Brief creative team	Susan	1 day
Develop creative approaches	Agency creative team	2 weeks
Review creative approaches	Susan	3 days
Select creative approach	Ed & Susan	1 day
Redefine budget with production estimates	Susan	2 days
Layouts	Agency art director	1 week
Brochure, ad & script copywriting	Agency copywriter	2 weeks
Review layout and copy	Susan	3 days
Revise layout and copy	Art director and copywriter	3 days
Secure company approvals	Susan	1 day
Secure product for photography	Susan	2 days
Hire photographer	Agency	1 day
Hire make-up stylist	Agency	15 minutes
Secure scenic locations	Agency	3-4 days
Secure facility locations	Susan	1-2 days
Schedule photography & video shoot	Agency	1 hour
Art direct & shoot photography	Art director & photographer	2 days
Process film	Photographer	3 days
Review & select photographs	Art director & Susan	1 day
Shoot video	Video company	3 days
Post production of video	Video company	2 weeks
Final layout & copy revise of ad & brochure	Art director and writer	3 days
Final layout and copy approval	Ed & Susan	2 days
Review video	Susan	1 day
Final edit video	Video company	1 week
Select printer	Susan	1 day
Reserve press time	Susan	15 minutes

Input final copy for artwork or typesetting	Agency	2 days
Scan photos	Printer	3 days
Prepare camera-ready art	Agency production artist	1 week
Read proofs of artwork	Ed & Susan	2 days
Revisions to artwork	Agency production artist	3 days
Final approval of artwork	Susan	1 day
Deliver art on disk to printer	Agency	1 day
Prepare film	Printer	2 days
Check preliminary color proofs of photos	Agency	1 day
Correct color	Printer	2 days
Approve final color	Agency	1 hour
Make blueline and composed color proof	Printer	2 days
Check & approve press proofs	Agency & Susan	1 day
Bindery	Printer	3 days
Shipping out of area	Printer	4 days

Assuming some of the tasks can be done at the same time, you have at least 16 to 20 weeks ahead of you to complete all of the materials you want. With this in mind you can evaluate the importance of each task and set the priorities that will help you meet your goals.

Step 2—Set Up the Job Organizer

In order to keep everything on track, it is a good idea to use the *job organizer form* (Figure 16.1). For the sake of the organizer, use preliminary budgets that have been gathered from potential suppliers by using the *request for preliminary estimate* (Figure 16.2). In this example the agency will select all of the suppliers, but you will review and approve the costs. The *request for video proposal form* (Figure 16.3) that is sent to the video company would be sent out by the agency but you can use the same form if you buy directly.

The costs used on the sample forms in this chapter are only examples and not representative of standard costs. Since so many factors affect costs, it is dangerous to provide accurate numbers as guidelines! Get real bids from suppliers. Then, once you have real costs, you can always go back later to verify that you are on budget or to change the numbers based on the direction the project is taking.

Figure 16.1   Job Organizer

Project: _New Widget Release Brochure, Video and Ad_

Project Number: _WR 90593_

Before you fill in the chart, note that not all tasks will have a cost and not all tasks may be required. Fill in the applicable information only.

Task	Cost Estimate	Due Date	Person/Company Responsible
Creative Development:			
Initial meeting with designer/agency		2/15	Susan Jones/Widget Works
Contact subs/vendors		4/24	Bright, Smart & Co.
Project estimate		2/28	Bright, Smart & Co.
Information gathering		2/15 to 4/5	Susan Jones
Information to designer/agency		4/5	Susan Jones
Information to copywriter		4/5	John Bright/Bright, Smart & Co.
Concept and initial layouts	3,750	4/20	Stan Torres/Bright, Smart & Co.
Copy and script	5,125	4/28	Julia Smith/Bright, Smart & Co.
Client approval of initial concepts		4/23	Bill Big & Susan Smith/Widget Works
Copy revisions		5/6	Stan Torres/B.S. & Co.
Final approval of copy		5/7	Susan Jones/WW
Final layouts	1,810	4/28	Stan Torres/B.S. & Co.
Client approval		5/4	Susan Jones/WW
Comprehensive layout		5/5	Stan Torres/B.S. & Co.
Client approval		5/6	Susan Jones/WW
Video pre-production:	4,800	4/12-4/24	Smith Film & Video

Figure 16.1   Job Organizer *(continued)*

Task	Cost Estimate	Due Date	Person/Company Responsible
Production:			
Video shooting and production	31,313	4/28	Smith Film & Video
Photography	4,050	5/8	Ansel Adman/Living Color
Art direction	1,360	5/8	Stan Torres/ B.S. & Co.
Illustration			
Mechanical artwork	1,665	5/13	Art Good/B.S. & Co.
Travel	1,100	5/7	Susan Jones, Stan Torres, Bill Bright
Artwork revisions		5/16	Art Good/ B.S. & Co.
Artwork final approval		5/17	Bill Big, Susan Jones/ WW
Video post production:	15,700		Smith Film & Video
Pre-press:	5,200		
Artwork to service bureau or printer		5/18	Lisa Garcia/XYZ Printer
Bluelines/color proofs		5/23	XYZ Printer
Revisions		5/25	Art Good/B.S. & Co.
Client approval		5/25	Susan Jones/WW
Film to printer (or to platemaking		5/25	XYZ Printer
Film for ad	6,650	5/25	Art Good/B.S. & Co.
Printing:			
Press check		5/28	Susan Jones/WW & John Smith (B.S. & Co.)
Printing to bindery		6/1	XYZ Printer
Delivery		6/4	XYZ Printer
Video duplication and delivery	2,520	6/4	Smith Film & Video

Figure 16.2   Request for Preliminary Estimates

FROM:

Name: *Susan Jones*

Company: *Widget Works, Inc.*

Address: *666 First St., Big Town, CA 90001*

Phone: *714 444-0000*   Ext.: *32*   Date: *4/24*

TO:

Name: *John Bright*

Company: *Bright, Smart & Co.*

Address: *1234 Main St., Small Town, CA 90000*

Phone: *714 555-6543*   Ext.: _____

Description of company services or products: _____
Advertising and graphic design
_____

Project Title: *Widget new product release*

Project description: *Marketing campaign*

   Item 1   *Full page, four color ad*

   Item 2   *8 page, 4 color brochure with photos*

   Item 3   *Video (see attached RFP)*

Proposal due date: *5/7*

Project due date: item 1 *6/30*   item 2 *7/22*   item 3 *8/15*

Overall budget: *$110,000*

Number of copies (or desired length):

   item 1 *2 sizes*   item 2 *10,000*   item 3 *7 to 10 minutes*

Level of quality: basic _____ good _____ best *X* superior _____

Description of tasks to be provided by supplier (i.e., photography, design, copywriting, printing, etc.) _____
Concept through production of all. Include 8 photos in brochure with one or two
also used in ad. Video and brochure photography to be shot on location in Tempe,
Arizona at manufacturing plant and in Orange County, California at corporate
office. Client to provide applicable research and background information. Client
and agency to select printer with agency supervising printing.

Figure 16.3   Request for Video Proposal

FROM: Widget Works, Inc.
CONTACT: Susan Jones
ADDRESS: 666 First St., Big Town, U.S.A., CA 90001
PHONE: 714 444-0000
DATE: 2/1

Situation Analysis:

- To enhance the image of the company through a new product launch and increase support of the distributors by providing easy to use sales materials
- Widget Works is preparing to release a new product in early June at the trade show in Atlanta. The product will be positioned against the competition's recent release of a slower but more ergonomically attractive product

Assignment:

Develop an 8 to 10 minute video for the first launch on June 12 to include:

- Full demonstration of new product and its features
- Sample applications of new product in different customer environments
- Brief history and background of Widget Works, demonstrating successful track record of other products

Target Audience:

Distributors and end-users.

Objectives:

- Introduce the customer to new product
- Create awareness of new product's value-added capabilities
- Create awareness of new product's competitive pricing

Strategies:

- Develop complete campaign to introduce new product through use of print ad, 8-page brochure and video. Campaign will include comprehensive coverage of key features and customer benefits of the new product
- Provide competitive comparison information to help elevate the product

(continued)

Figure 16.3   Request for Video Proposal (continued)

Rationale:

As Widget Works prepares to launch a new product, it is important to provide every sales tool possible. The campaign must reflect the progressive approach that has always given Widget Works its reputation as an industry leader. The video will provide excellent media to do this.

Bid/Budget:

To include all of the following:

- All shooting of film (include 3 location shots of manufacturing plant at Tempe, Arizona)
- Stock film (if applicable)
- Animation of product rotating and dropping into housing
- Studio/equipment rental
- Talent payments
- Post production—editing, music, special effects
- Creation of master and sub-master
- Dubbing and shipping of 400 videotapes to distributors

Do not include the following:

- Script fee (agency to provide)

Budget:

The budget on this bid will be fixed. It may not exceed $70,000. This project will not have any contingency on the budget.

Schedule:

Request for Proposal	2/1
Bid from production company	3/3
Award job	3/5
Script to client	3/20
Final script	4/10
Pre-production	4/12–4/24
Begin production	4/27
Edit/Dupe	5/9
Client review	5/10
Final edit/Dupe	5/15
Dupe/Collate	5/20–5/24
Delivery (Ship 3 day)	6/4

Step 3—Select the Suppliers

Since it would be difficult to fill in the job organizer completely without having suppliers lined up, set it aside temporarily. For the sake of this example, assume that you have narrowed the field of potential agencies to three finalists by reviewing their qualifications and initial *cost estimates* (Figures 16.4, 16.5 & 16.6) for the work you need done. Remember, it is difficult to provide accurate costs until concepts and initial layouts are finalized. The preliminary estimates will help your decision in selecting your agency. Later, the agency will provide final cost estimates based on approved concepts.

Now you want to get down to business and make a selection. Pull out the *evaluation form* (Figure 16.7) for selecting agencies. Once you have completed your review, fill in the *finalist comparison form* (Figure 16.8). Evaluate the importance of each item. Although one firm may score high in one area, it may not be the one that is most important to you. In addition to the evaluations, review the initial quotations for the cost of performing the work you need done. Now make your decision.

Based on the evaluation form and quotation results (and your gut feelings), Bright, Smart & Co. will be your new agency. Since this is your first project with them you may not be ready to sign a retainer agreement. However, you do need to fill out and sign the *service contract* (Figure 16.9).

Once layouts for the brochure are approved, you will be ready to get final printing estimates. If you want to select your own printer rather than have the agency do it, don't forget that you take responsibility for the results! If you feel comfortable working with the printer, use the *printer specification sheet* (Figure 16.10) and the *printer evaluation form* (Figure 16.11) to help keep your thinking organized. Now go back to your organizer and finish filling it in.

Figure 16.4 Video Script and Ad Cost Estimate

Please fill out completely. Use a different form for each separate project.

Company: *Bright, Smart & Co.*

Contact person: *John Bright*

Address: *1234 Main St., Small Town, CA 90000*

Phone: *714 987-6543*   Ext.: _____   Date: *5/5*

Client: *Widget Works, Inc.*

Project description: *Full page, four color ad for new widget. Includes two initial concepts, one revised concept and one final layout utilizing two photos from brochure photo session. Also includes two same size sets of film and proofs shipped to publications. Artwork provided on disk. Also cost of one 7 to 10 minute video script.*

Project Management Costs:

Research	*N/A*
Meetings and coordination	*750.00*

Creative Costs:

Concept and initial layout	*1,750.00*
Final layout	*750.00*
Production art	*625.00*
Copywriting	*750.00*
Video script	*2,500.00*
Art direction*	*N/A*
Illustration	*N/A*
Subtotal	*7,126.00*

Figure 16.4   Video Script and Ad Cost Estimate *(continued)*

Supplier Costs *(fill out the applicable information only)*:

Photography*	_____
Film and processing	_____
Props	_____
Stylist	_____
Typesetting	_____
Computer output (to paper)	*10.00*
Film and proofs	*1,650.00*

Miscellaneous costs:

Travel *(explain)* _____	
_____	_____
Copies	*5.00*
Delivery	*26.00*
Cartage	_____
Other *(explain)* _____	
_____	_____
Subtotal	*1,691.00*
Taxable total	*8,817.00*
Sales tax	*683.33*
TOTAL	*9,500.32*

* *Photography costs included with brochure.*

Figure 16.5   Brochure Cost Estimate

Company: *Bright, Smart & Co.*

Contact person: *John Bright*

Address: *1234 Main St., Small Town, CA 90000*

Phone: *714 987-6543* _____ Ext.: _____ Date: *5/5*

Project description: *Eight page, four color, 11" x 17" brochure (folding to 8.5" x 11") for new widget, with 8 photos, quantity 10,000 on 80# Encore Gloss Coated Cover Stock. Includes 2 initial concepts, one final layout, one full day photography and art direction on site in Tempe, Arizona and one day in Orange County, CA. and production art. Artwork provided on disk to printer.*

Project Management Costs:

Research	*N/A*
Meetings and coordination	*750.00*

Creative Costs:

Concept and initial layout	*2,000.00*
Final layout	*1,060.00*
Production art	*1,040.00*
Copywriting	*1,875.00*
Art direction	*1,360.00*
Illustration	*N/A*
Subtotal	*4,626.00*

Supplier Costs *(fill out the applicable information only):*

Photography	*3,500.00*
Film and processing	*550.00*

Figure 16.5   Brochure Cost Estimate *(continued)*

Computer output *(to paper)* ___*24.00*___

Color output
  (for final layouts)   ___*300.00*___

Printing *(includes scans, film and final proofs)**

  Quantity 1   ___*11,950.00*___

  Quantity 2 ___*13,425.00*___

  Quantity 3 ___*14,780.00*___

    Subtotal   ___*16,324.00*___

Miscellaneous costs:

  Travel *(explain)* _____
  2 round-trip tickets to
  Tempe and one day car
  rental   ___*750.00*___

  Copies   ___*25.00*___

  Delivery   ___*N/A*___

  Cartage   _____

  Other *(explain)* _____

  _____   _____

Subtotal   ___*775.00*___

Taxable total   ___*20,975.00*___

Non-taxable total   ___*750.00*___

Sales tax   ___*1,625.56*___

TOTAL   ___*23,350.56*___

* *Estimates only, final costs to provided upon approval of final layout*

Figure 16.6 Film and Video Production Estimate

Agency: Bright, Smart & Company
Production company: Smith Film and Video Co.

Name: _____
Name: _____

Address: 1234 Mainstreet
Address: 45678 Mainstreet

City, State, Zip: Small Town, CA 90000
City, State, Zip: Anywhere, U.S.A.

Phone: (714) 987-6343
Phone: (654) 765-4321

Fax: (714) 987-6340
Fax: (654) 765-4322

Client: Widget Works, Inc.
Producer: Bill Smith

Title: "Into the 21st Century"
Writer: Word Smith

Agency contact: John Bright
Director: Jane Smith

Client contact: Susan Jones
Editor: Billy Smith

Bid date: January 1, 19xx
File name: C:\bids\XYZCO

Summary of estimated costs

Pre-production and wrap costs	Total A&C	4,800
Shooting crew labor	Total B	11,520
Location and Travel expense	Total D	612
Props and Wardrobe	Total E	100
Studio expenses	Total F	3,220
Set Construction	Total G&H	2,800
Equipment costs	Total I	5,130
Raw Stock, Develop and Transfer	Total J	300
Miscellaneous	Total K	250
Sub-Total A–K		28,732
Director/Creative fees	Total L	7,381
Sub-Total Direct Costs		36,113
Production Fee		12,640
Talent	Total M&N	4,786
Post Production	Total O	15,700

Total Estimate	69,247

Figure 16.6   Film and Video Production Estimate *(continued)*

Crew:	A: Pre-pro/Wrap				B: Pre-light/shoot			
	Days	Rate	O.T.	Total		Days	Rate	O.T.	Total
Executive Producer	1	500	0	500		0	0	0	0
Producer	2	350	0	1,750		2	350	0	700
Coordinator	0	0	0	0		0	0	0	0
Assistant Director	0	0	0	0		0	0	0	0
Cinematographer	0	0	0	0		2	950	0	1,900
Video Engineer	0	0	0	0		2	300	0	600
Art Director	1	500	0	500		2	500	0	1,000
Prop Master	0	0	0	0		0	0	0	0
Gaffer	0	0	0	0		2	400	0	800
Best Boy	0	0	0	0		2	300	0	600
Electrician	0	0	0	0		0	0	0	0
Electrician	0	0	0	0		0	0	0	0
Key Grip	0	0	0	0		2	400	0	800
Best Boy	0	0	0	0		2	300	0	600
Grip	0	0	0	0		0	0	0	0
Grip	0	0	0	0		0	0	0	0
Audio Mixer	0	0	0	0		2	450	0	900
Boom Operator	0	0	0	0		0	0	0	0
Make Up	0	0	0	0		2	400	0	800
Hair	0	0	0	0		0	0	0	0
Wardrobe	0	0	0	0		0	0	0	0
Script Clerk	0	0	0	0		2	450	0	900
Home Economist	0	0	0	0		0	0	0	0
Video Assist Oper	0	0	0	0		0	0	0	0
Special Effects	0	0	0	0		0	0	0	0
Teleprompter	0	0	0	0		0	0	0	0
Location Scout	1	250	0	250		0	0	0	0
Production Asst.	0	0	0	0		0	0	0	0
Craft Service	0	0	0	0		0	0	0	0
Helicopter Pilot	0	0	0	0		0	0	0	0
Aerial Cameraman	0	0	0	0		0	0	0	0
Policemen	0	0	0	0		0	0	0	0
Fireman	0	0	0	0		0	0	0	0
Medical Tech.	0	0	0	0		0	0	0	0
Teacher/Welfare	0	0	0	0		0	0	0	0
	0	0	0	0		0	0	0	0
	0	0	0	0		0	0	0	0

Sub-Total A	3,000	Sub-Total B	9,600
PT/P&W	600	PT/P&W	1,920
Total A	3,600	Total B	11,520

(continued)

Figure 16.6 Film and Video Production Estimate *(continued)*

C: Pre-production and wrap costs	No.	Days	Rate	Total
Auto Rentals	0	0	0	0
Air fares	0	0	0	0
Per-Diem	0	0	0	0
Still Camera, film & processing	1	2	50	100
Deliveries	0	0	0	0
Trucking	0	0	0	0
Casting director	1	1	600	600
Casting facilities	1	1	500	500
Working meals	0	0	0	0
	0	0	0	0
			Total C	1,200

D: Location Expenses	No.	Days	Rate	Total
Location fees	1	1	250	250
Permits	1	1	50	50
Tracking	0	0	0	0
Mileage	0	0	0	0
Motorhome	0	0	0	0
Car prep. & Transport	0	0	0	0
Vehicle rental	0	0	0	0
Airfare	0	0	0	0
Airfreight	0	0	0	0
Hotels	0	0	0	0
Per-Diem	0	0	0	0
Craft Service	1	12	8	96
Meals	1	12	18	216
Security guards	0	0	0	0
	0	0	0	0
			Total D	612

E: Props, Wardrobe & Animals	No.	Rate	Total
Prop purchase/rental	1	100	100
Wardrobe purchase/rental	0	0	0
Picture Vehicles	0	0	0
Animals & Handlers	0	0	0
		Total E	100

Figure 16.6   Film and Video Production Estimate *(continued)*

F: Studio Rental and Expense	No.	Days	Rate	Total
Build days	1	1	750	750
Pre-light days	0	0	0	0
Shoot days	1	1	1,200	1,200
Wrap days	0	0	0	0
Stage manager	1	1	250	250
Power/Generator	1	10	45	450
Phones, coffee, etc.	1	1	50	50
Craft service	1	20	8	160
Meals	1	20	18	360
	0	0	0	0
			Total F	3,220

G: Set Construction	No.	Rate	Total
Set Designer	0	0	0
Set Construction crew	1	1,800	1,800
Tracking	1	500	500
Mileage	0	0	0
Set Wrap	0	0	0
	0	0	0
	0	0	0
		Total G	2,300

H: Set Construction Materials	No.	Rate	Total
Set purchase	0	0	0
Materials	1	500	500
Set Rentals	0	0	0
Trucking & Mileage	0	0	0
Special Effects	0	0	0
	0	0	0
Prop rental	0	0	0
Prop Purchase	0	0	0
	0	0	0
	0	0	0
	0	0	0
		Total H	500

(continued)

Figure 16.6 Film and Video Production Estimate *(continued)*

I: Equipment Rental	No.	Days	Rate	Total
Camera Equipment	1	2	650	1,300
Special Lenses	0	0	0	0
Audio Equipment	1	2	50	100
Grip truck and equipment	1	2	450	900
Mileage	100	2	0.45	90
Lighting equipment	1	2	750	1,500
Generator & delivery	1	1	450	450
Camera car	0	0	0	0
Dolly/Crane	1	2	145	290
Car Mounts	0	0	0	0
Video assist/Monitors	0	0	0	0
Helicopter	0	0	0	0
Teleprompter	0	0	0	0
Walkie Talkies	0	0	0	0
Supplies and Expendables	1	2	250	500
			Total I	5,130

J: Raw Stock, Develop, Transfer	No.	Rate	Total
Film stock	0	0	0
Film Processing	0	0	0
Audio tape	0	0	0
Audio transfers	0	0	0
Video Tape	10	30	300
Film to tape transfers	0	0	0
Stock for video transfer	0	0	0
Off-line copies	0	0	0
Transfer supervision	0	0	0
	0	0	0
		Total J	300

K: Miscellaneous	No.	Rate	Total
Petty cash	2	50	100
Phones/Faxes	2	50	100
Shipping	0	0	0
Deliveries	1	50	50
Insurance	0	0	0
		Total K	250

Figure 16.6   Film and Video Production Estimate *(continued)*

L: Director/Creative fees	No.	Days	Rate	Total
Research	1	1	500	500
Writing	1	1	2,500	2,500
Storyboards	1	1	500	500
Director's Prep Days	1	2	350	700
Director's Travel Days	0	0	0	0
Director's Shoot Days	1	2	750	1,500
Director's Post Days	1	1	350	350
	0	0	0	0
	0	0	0	0
		Sub-Total L		6,050
		PT/P&W		1,331
			Total L	7,381

M: Talent	No.	Days	Rate	OT/Travel	Total
Principal talent	1	2	396	0	792
Principal talent	0	0	0	0	0
Narrators	0	0	0	0	0
Extras	0	0	0	0	0
Extras	5	2	150	0	1,500
Stuntmen	0	0	0	0	0
Precision drivers	0	0	0	0	0
Hand models	0	0	0	0	0
	0	0	0	0	0
		Sub-Total M			2,292
				PT/P&W	917
		Handling Fee			1,284
				Total M	4,492

N: Talent Expenses	No.	Days	Rate	Total
Travel: Mileage, airfare, etc.	100	2	0.25	50
Hotel, Per-Diem	1	1	145	145
Wardrobe Allowance	1	1	15	15
	0	0	0	0
		Sub-Total N		210
		Handling Fee		84
			Total N	294

(continued)

Figure 16.6 Film and Video Production Estimate *(continued)*

O: Post-Production	No.	Rate	Total
Graphics	1	400	400
Animation	1	1,500	1,500
Music	1	750	750
Narration recording	2	95	190
Sound Effects	1	100	100
Audio transfers	2	75	150
Audio lay-down/lay-back	2	50	100
Audio sweetening	6	250	1,500
Digitizing	4	95	380
Off-line	16	125	2,000
Lay off — dubs & delivery	1	75	75
Re-digitizing	0	0	0
2nd Cut off-line	0	0	0
Lay-off dubs & delivery	0	0	0
On-line	8	225	1,800
ADO	0	0	0
Chyron	0	0	0
Matte Camera	0	0	0
	0	0	0
Sub-Masters	0	0	0
Edit Master	1	75	75
Protection Master	0	0	0
Duplication Master	0	0	0
Dubs & delivery	1	75	75
	0	0	0
Mass Duplication	400	2.25	900
Labels	400	.45	180
Packaging	400	1	400
Assembly	400	.25	100
Shipping	400	2.35	940
	0	0	0
Delivery Service (FedEx, UPS, etc.)	0	0	0
	0	0	0
	0	0	0
			0
	Sub-Total O		11,615
	Handling Fee		4,093
	Total O		15,700

Figure 16.7a   Evaluation Form

Company: _Hollis & Hollis Advertising_

Contact: _Evelyn Hollis_ _____ Phone no.: _(714) 555-0000_

No. of employees: _8_ _____ Years in business: _7_

Rate each of the following on a scale of 1 to 10, 10 being the highest.

Work samples

Creativity	7
Neatness	10
Originality	6
Effectiveness	7
Similarity to your needs	8
Style	8
Versatility	5

Professionalism

Organizational skills	9
References	9
Personal appearance(s)	10
Punctuality	10
Presentation techniques	10
Communication skills	9

Staff

Related experience	6
Level of comfort with contact	9
Management skills	9
TOTAL	133

Additional comments: _The presentation was very strong but the work lacked in creativity. Everything looked the same no matter who the client was._

Figure 16.7b Evaluation Form

Company: *Bright, Smart & Co.*

Contact: *John Bright*   Phone no.: *(714) 555-6543*

No. of employees: *12*   Years in business: *8*

Rate each of the following on a scale of 1 to 10, 10 being the highest.

Work samples

Creativity	*8*
Neatness	*10*
Originality	*8*
Effectiveness	*8*
Similarity to your needs	*9*
Style	*8*
Versatility	*7*

Professionalism

Organizational skills	*10*
References	*10*
Personal appearance(s)	*10*
Punctuality	*10*
Presentation techniques	*7*
Communication skills	*8*

Staff

Related experience	*10*
Level of comfort with contact	*7*
Management skills	*8*
TOTAL	*138*

Additional comments: *Strong experience in the area we need. Account executive assigned to our account weak in market area but President strong. Unusual solutions with excellent results. Offered new approach with good strategic thinking.*

Figure 16.7c   Evaluation Form

Company: _The Creative Co._

Contact: _Jason Smith_ _____ Phone no.: _(714) 555-1111_

No. of employees: __3__ _____ Years in business: __2__

Rate each of the following on a scale of 1 to 10, 10 being the highest.

Work samples

Creativity	10
Neatness	6
Originality	10
Effectiveness	6
Similarity to your needs	8
Style	9
Versatility	9

Professionalism

Organizational skills	7
References	9
Personal appearance(s)	8
Punctuality	10
Presentation techniques	10
Communication skills	9

Staff

Related experience	7
Level of comfort with contact	7
Management skills	8

TOTAL __134__

Additional comments: _Although they seem highly creative with innovative ideas, they were a bit disorganized. They were not sure of the results of their prior campaigns. Possibly not marketing-oriented enough for our needs._

Figure 16.8 Finalist Comparisons

A. Name: _The Creative Co._   Phone: _(714) 555-1111_

B. Name: _Hollis & Hollis Advertising_   Phone: _(714) 555-0000_

C. Name: _Bright, Smart & Co._   Phone: _(714) 555-6543_

Rate each of the following on a scale of 1 to 10, with 10 as the highest rating.

	A	B	C
Work samples			
Creativity	10	7	8
Neatness	6	10	10
Originality	10	6	8
Effectiveness	6	7	8
Similarity to your needs	8	8	9
Style	9	8	8
Versatility	9	5	7
Professionalism			
Organizational skills	7	9	10
References	9	9	10
Personal appearance(s)	8	10	10
Punctuality	10	10	10
Presentation techniques	10	10	7
Communication skills	9	9	8
Staff			
Related experience	7	6	10
Level of comfort with contact	7	9	7
Management skills	8	9	8
TOTAL	134	133	138

Figure 16.9   Sample Service Contract

Date: _2/15_

Client: _Widget Works_

Client Address: _666 First St., Big Town, USA, CA 90001_

Client Phone #: _714 444-0000_

Project: _New Product Release Ad, Brochure & Video_

From (designer or agency contact): _Bill Bright_

Estimated Total Cost: (see attached estimate) $ _108,000_

Terms: _30_ % of all art charges will be invoiced upon approval of estimate. _30% of video charges due upon approval of script_ . Remainder of all art charges to be invoiced upon delivery of final artwork. _50_ % of film and printing to be billed upon release of artwork to printer. Balance of film and printing to be billed upon delivery of printed materials. Balance of video charges due upon delivery of master. If the project is not completed within two weeks of the date of the final invoice, all outstanding charges will be billed at that time. In adherence to trade customs and procedures, liability for any errors, except those of a technical nature related to the printing process, rests with the client once approvals for finished artwork have been signed off by the client.

Payment Schedule: All invoices are due _10_ days from date of invoice.

Termination: If work is terminated by either party before completion of this project, all fees plus supplier expenses will be billable up to the point of termination. Losses caused by the termination of thie contract (such as liabilities for reserved advertising space or scheduling of suppliers), shall be paid by the client.

Ownership: the client has the following rights to the artwork and copywriting created in this project: _All photography and original video footage will be owned by the photographer, Ansel Adman and video production company, Smith Film and Video Company. All artwork and copywriting will be owned by the client, Widget Works, Inc._

All rights not expressly granted in this agreement remain the exclusive property of the designer (or copywriter or agency). Artwork created for use in this project by the vendors (i.e., illustrators, photographers) of the designer/agency is the property of those vendors and may not be used without permission. The approved usage beyond the scope of this project will be billed at prevailing rates unless otherwise predetermined. Full rights and usage will be determined and agreed upon in writing. Client shall return all artwork within 60 days from completion of project.

Press proofs: Unless the client is present when the plate is made ready for the press, so that no press time is lost, presses standing waiting the approval of the customer will be charged at current rated for the time consumed. If the client chooses not to be at the press check, XYZ Agency will not be held responsible for the approval of the press sheet.

(continued)

Figure 16.9 Sample Service Contract *(continued)*

Overruns and Underruns: Due to the nature of printing, up to a 10% variance of quantity may occur. The client will be billed according to the exact quantity that is delivered.

Additional Charges: This agreement is based on the project and services described in the attached estimate. It does not include charges for revisions due to changes requested by the client in the scope or design of the project as described; if such changes are necessary, they will be estimated in advance and billed separately, and the client agrees to pay such charges. Suppliers' charges are approximate pending final approval of layout and copy. The client will be notified, in writing, of any changes in these portions of the estimate.

Expenses: Mileage, long-distance telephone calls, photocopies, postage, messenger services, and cartage are not included and will be billed in addition to the charges above. These charges will not exceed $100 without prior client approval. Travel charges (airfare, hotel, etc.) related to the job will be billed additionally.

Scheduling: The designer/agency is not responsible for meeting the production schedule should the client fail to provide the required materials to complete the project based on that schedule.

Production Schedule: The production schedule is due as follows: concept and initial layouts _4/20_, final layouts _4/28_, final copy _5/6_, production art _5/13_, printing _6/4_, other (describe) _Video. 6/4_.

Note: If work does not begin on this project within 30 days, we are permitted to submit revised estimates reflecting any cost changes. If work begun is subsequently delayed, or place on hold, the project will be re-estimated to reflect prevailing costs before continuing.

Please indicate your approval by signing and returning one copy. Your signature gives _Bright, Smart & Company_ the authority to undertake the work described in this estimate and to bill in accordance with the terms stated. Your signature also indicated your acceptance of all costs, terms, and provisions of this estimate. In the event that litigation occurs due to any aspect of the project, the losing party agrees to pay all court and attorney fees.

Duly signed by an authorized agent.

Name: _Susan Jones_   Date: _2/15_

Company: _Widget Works_   Title: _Advertising Manager_

Name: _Bill Bright_   Date: _2/15_

Company: _Bright, Smart & Co._   Title: _Senior Account Executive_

Figure 16.10 Printer Specification Sheet

Fill out a separate form for each piece.

Company: *Widget Works, Inc.*   Date: *5/12*

Contact: *Susan Jones*

Address: *666 First St., Big Town, CA 90001*

Phone: *714 444-0000*   FAX: *714 444-0001*

Printer Name: *XYZ Printing, Inc.*   Contact: *Lisa Garcia*

Address: *1234 Long St., Big Town, CA 90001*

Phone: *714 444-9876*   FAX: *714 444-9876*

Job Name: *Widget new product release*   Job No.: *NPR50799*

Job Description: *Product brochure*   Date Due: *6/4*

Quantity: 1) *5,000* 2) *10,000* 3) *15,000* Additional/m's: *yes*

Size: Flat *17"* x *11"* Folded/Bound *8.5"* x *11"*

No. of pages: *8*   Self-cover *X*   Plus cover _____

Art provided as:

Disk (type) *Macintosh* Program *Quark* Version *3.32*

Artboard _____

Composed film with proofs _____ Loose film _____

Printer to prepare _____

Number of inks: Cover side one *4* Cover side two *4*

Inside side one *4* Inside side two *4*

Special inks and or varnish: *NO*

Number of separations and sizes:

From transparencies *1 – 8" × 10", 4 – 5" × 7" and 3 – 2" × 3"*

From reflective _____

(continued)

Figure 16.10 Printer Specification Sheet *(continued)*

Number of halftones and sizes:

Halftones _____

Duotones _____

Photo special effects (Mezzotints, line conversions, etc.): _____

_____

Photo alterations (Outlines, vignettes, retouch): _____
_____ *Drop out background in 2 photos*

Stock:	Weight	Name	Finish	Color	Grade
Cover	*80#*	*Encore*	*Gloss*	*White*	*Cover*
Inside	*80#*	*Encore*	*Gloss*	*White*	*Cover*

Fold type: *Standard* _____

Bindery:

Flat ___ Collate & gather ___ Punch ___ Drill Score/perforate _×_

Pad ___ Saddle stitch ___ Paste bind ___ Perfect bind ___ GVC ___

Wire-O ___ Spiral bound ___ Case bound ___ Tip in ___

Special (i.e., emboss, foil, die-cut, number, etc.): _____
_____ *Emboss (2" × 5")*

Packing instructions: *Cartons* _____

Delivery: *F.O.B. Big Town, CA* _____

Additional information: _____
_____ *Allow for bleed on front cover only and traps*

_____

_____

_____

Figure 16.11   Printer Evaluation Form

Date _____5/10_____

Name of Company _____XYZ Printing, Inc._____

Address _____1234 Long St., Big Town, CA 90001_____

_____

Phone _____714 444-9876_____   FAX _____714 444-9877_____

Contact _____Lisa Garcia_____

Title _____Rep_____

Type of printer: __ quick __ small _×_ Mid-size __ Large __ Specialty

Rate the following 1-10 (10 being premium or best)

_____9_____ Quality   _____8_____ Pre-press capabilities

_____10_____ Service   _____8_____ Proofing capabilities

_____9_____ Shop appearance   _____0_____ Art department

_____10_____ Reputation   _____9_____ Samples

Sheetfed offset press descriptions:

Brand _Heidelberg_ Max. Sheet Size _26"_ Min. Sheet Size ____ # Colors _4_

Brand _____ Max. Sheet Size ____ Min. Sheet Size ____ # Colors ____

Brand _____ Max. Sheet Size ____ Min. Sheet Size ____ # Colors ____

Brand _____ Max. Sheet Size ____ Min. Sheet Size ____ # Colors ____

Web offset press descriptions:

Brand _____ Maximum Roll Width _____ Cut-off _____ # Colors ____

Brand _____ Maximum Roll Width _____ Cut-off _____ # Colors ____

Additional capabilities (i.e., die cut, foil stamp, embossing, engraving, thermography)

_____ In-house Kluge for die-cut and foil _____

_____

_____

(continued)

Figure 16.11   Printer Evaluation Form *(continued)*

Area of specialization   *Small to medium run 2 to 4 color*

Describe capabilities, limitations, and equipment available:

Cutting   *Oversized sent out*

Folding   *In-house unless hand work*

Binding (i.e., wire, saddle stitch, staple, perfect, case, etc.)
None in-house except stitch and staple

Art department   *None*

Pre-press services   *Scitex and MacIntosh*

Delivery   *Own trucks*

Storage   *Limited*

Credit terms   *Net 30*

Scheduling procedures   *2 weeks advance to reserve press*

Previous customer references   *Jan at Smart Co. 714 455-9999*

Comments   *Very professional attitude. Samples exceptional
for size of shop. Watch pricing because of limited
in-house capabilities. Recently switched to
electronic pre-press so still learning curve.*

Step 4—Manage the Project

You shouldn't need any more forms at this point. Just keep referring back to your job organizer to ensure that your deadlines and cost estimates match what is actually happening and each person with a responsibility is following through. If you have been doing a good job of doing that, you shouldn't have any big surprises that you are not prepared for.

Remember, there isn't anything you can't get done. This *is* always someone out there who knows what to do when you don't and you *can* find them.

GLOSSARY

accordion fold In binding, a term used to describe a series of parallel folds, each opening opposite the next, similar to the pleats in an accordion

account coordinator The account coordinator assists the account executive with the coordination of projects in advertising agencies or graphic design firms.

account executive The account executive represents an advertising agency or design firm as a sales person and a liaison between the agency and client.

acetate A transparent sheet made of flexible clear plastic, frequently used to make overlays on mechanicals.

aerial cameraman The aerial cameraman is especially skilled to operate a camera and shoot from the air, usually in a helicopter.

airbrush A small pressure gun, shaped like a pencil that sprays watercolor pigment by means of compressed air. It is used to correct halftones and to obtain tone or graduated tone effects. It's also used with an abrasive pumice-like material to remove spots or other unwanted areas.

amberlith A red- or orange-coated brand of acetate that can be stripped. It is then cut and peeled away selectively to create outlines and silhouettes on art boards.

art director A person whose responsibilities include the creation of visual work and the talent to produce it, the purchase of visual work, and the supervision of the quality and character of the work. The art director is usually an employee of an advertising agency, publishing house, magazine, or other user of graphic artists' work, although some organizations hire free-lance art directors to perform these duties.

artwork A general term used to describe photographs, drawings, paintings, hand lettering, and the like, prepared to illustrate printed matter.

assistant cameraman The assistant cameraman is responsible for the set-up and operation of the camera. He is a technical person with a great deal of responsibility since mistakes can be very costly.

assistant director An assistant director is included in a video production if there is a large set, a lot of extras and the director needs help in controlling it.

audio lay-back The transferring back to the original master tape of sweetened audio sections.

audio lay-down The transferring of audio sections from the completed, edited videotape to the format proper for sweetening.

audio mixer The audio mixer is the sound recordist, whether on video or film. He mixes the sounds from the various microphones and monitors the quality of the recorded audio.

base color A first color used on a background on which other colors are printed.

basis weight The weight in pounds of a ream (500 sheets) of paper cut to a given standard size for that grade. For example, 500 sheets of 25" × 38" of 80-pound coated stock will weigh 80 pounds.

best boy (electrician) The assistant to the Gaffer is the best boy. He coordinates with the electrical crew to run the power to the lighting units, set them in the proper place and adjust them for the desired effect.

betacam   A high-quality ½" VTR format, such as VHS or F-VHS.

blanket   In offset lithography, the rubber-surfaced sheet clamped around the cylinder on the press, which transfers the image from the plate to paper.

blanket contamination   Foreign matter, such as dust or paper lint, that becomes attached to the blanket and interferes with the quality of printing.

bleed   An illustration or type is said to bleed when it prints off the edge of a trimmed page. Bleed illustrations are usually imposed so as to print beyond the trimmed page size. An illustration may bleed at the head, front, foot, or gutter of a page.

blind embossing   A technique in which a bas-relief is stamped without foil or ink.

blowup   An enlargement of the original size.

boards   Artwork and text (type-set copy) pasted up on boards. Also, a variety of paperboards used for packaging, boxes and cartons.

boom operator   The boom operator handles the placement of microphones in order to obtain the best sound pick-up and quality.

break for color   In artwork preparation and composition, to separate by color the elements to be printed in different colors. Copy and art for each color are pasted on separate sheets, or overlays.

bug   A term used to describe a trademark or logo.

build   A build day on a stage is a construction day for the set construction crew.

burn   An exposure made with an arc lamp in the platemaking process.

burn out   To overexpose in such a way on a press plate that no tints come up.

buyout   The payment of a fee for artwork for the sale of *all rights,* and sometimes for the original art itself, is agreed to by the artist. This term is usually used in advertising.

CLC (caps and lower case)   The type style usually used for headings or titles, consisting of type in which only the first letter of each major word is capitalized.

C-print   Intermediate negative full-color positive print from a negative transparency.

C-stands (Century stands)   Lighting stands that hold scrims, silks and flags in position are called C-stands.

camera-ready art   Material (text, artwork, illustrations and photographs) given to the printer that needs no further work before being passed on to the camera department. Camera-copy should be clean, flat, and printed in dark ink.

caps   All type fonts have capital letters for emphasis; they are sometimes referred to as "upper case."

casting call (cattle call)   A notice sent out to talent agents of a session to select talent for a particular role in a film or video production.

casting director   The casting director is in charge of locating and selecting the talent for the video or film production.

casting facility   A room or rooms where a casting session may take place is the casting facility. The talent comes together at this location to be reviewed by the production company, the director and the casting director.

Chromalin proofs   A proprietary term for a color proofing process that employs a photosensitized clear plastic upon which images are made from color separation film negatives. Such proofs are used for presentations and for checking register, obvious blemishes, and size.

chyron   The titling device which superimposes the titles across the bottom of a scene.

cinematographer (or videographer)   The cinematographer (for film) or the videographer (for video) is responsible for the visual look of the project which includes the lighting and composition. Sometimes they operate the cameras themselves, other times they direct the camera operator and concentrate on the design of the lighting. This person is one of the most important people on the crew.

clip art   General illustrations, figures, and designs that can be purchases copyright free for use in mechanicals when the use of an artist is too costly.

close register   Used to describe low trap allowance, requiring more press printing positioning accuracy. Because each color is printed from a separate plate, the register, or positioning, of the plates must be exact to achieve a sharp image in the correct position.

CMYK   The abbreviation for the four colors of ink used in four-color process printing—cyan, magenta, yellow and black (key).

color bars   On four-color process proofs, samples of the color used to print the image. Color bars show the amount of ink used, the trapping, and the relative densities across the press sheet.

color coding   The use of different color stock, tinting, or printed marks on individual parts of a set to aid in identification and distribution.

color electronic scanner   Equipment used to make color separations by photoelectrically reading the relative densities of the copy.

color key   An overlay proof composed of an individual acetate sheet for each color.

color matching system   Method of specifying color by means of numbered color samples in swatchbooks.

color process   A reproduction of color made by means of photographic separations. The printing is done using cyan, magenta, yellow, and black inks, each requiring its own negative. Also called *process color* and *four-color process.*

color proofs   The first full-color printed pieces pulled off the press for approval before the job is considered ready to roll for the entire press run. Progressive proofs (or "progs") are the preferred method for checking color accurately.

color separation The process of separating full-color originals into the primary printing colors in negative or positive form. In lithographic platemaking, the manual separations of color are done by handwork performed directly on the printing surface. An artist can preseparate by using separate overlays for each color.

color swatch A small spot of color used to furnish a sample of the actual ink color to be produced.

color transparency A full-color transparent positive on a transparent support. Also called a chrome. Most often provided by photographers.

composite Several pictures, line or tone, placed together to form a single, combined picture.

composition The assembling of characters into words, lines, and paragraphs of text or body matter type for reproduction by printing.

comprehensive (or comp) A rough visualization of the idea for an illustration or design, usually created for the client and artist to use as a guide to the finished art. "Tight comp" or "loose comp" refers to the degree of detail, rendering, and general accuracy used in the comprehensive.

Compugraphic A manufacturer of typesetting equipment.

condensed face (or condensed type) A typeface designed to set tighter than normal, thus permitting a greater number of characters to fit a given measure.

contact proof A color proof made by exposing the film used for making printing plates directly to a special material.

contact print A print made by placing the negative in direct contact with the emulsion to generate a photographic print on paper.

continuous form Form manufactured from a continuous web that is not cut into units prior to execution.

continuous zone   Describes an image that has not been screened and contains gradient tones from black to white.

contrast   The density difference (total gradations) between the highlight and shadow area of copy; also called *copy density range,* as measured with a densitometer.

coordinator   The coordinator assists the video producer on larger job.

copy fitting   The adjustment of typeset copy to the space allotted by changing the space allotment, the copy length, the type size, the word spacing or the letter spacing.

copywriter   Writers are involved with the creation of concepts and writing of copy for marketing communication tools produced in print or electronic media.

cover paper (stock)   A term for a wide variety of papers durable enough to be used as covers on catalogs, pamphlets, booklets and the like.

craft service   The crafts, including all of the crew people and talent, need to be taken care of throughout the day or night with snacks or refreshments. The craft service person takes care of this responsibility.

crane   A long arm that the camera can be mounted on so it can be moved into position for photography.

creative director   Usually an employee or officer of an advertising agency whose responsibilities may include overall supervision of all aspects of the character and quality of the agency's work for its clients. The creative director's background may be in art, copy, or client contact.

credit line   A line of type, usually placed beneath or at the side of an illustration or other matter, giving credit to the owner, photographer, or artist. Credits for permission to reprint copyrighted material are sometimes listed on the copyright acknowledgement page.

crop   To trim an image or eliminate portions of copy.

crop marks Marks along the margins of an illustration, used to indicate the portion of the illustration to be reproduced.

cut A cut is an abrupt change from one scene to another, such as; from a wide to a narrow shot or from an exterior to an interior shot.

cut-size Papers cut for printing, copying, and business purposes.

Day-Glo Trade name for inks and papers containing fluorescent pigments.

debossing A process in which an image is pressed down into the paper surface; differs from embossing, which is a raised image.

deckle Normally a text paper with an edge that is irregular in outline and that decreases in thickness. Frequently used for announcements or high-quality booklets. Made in cover or text weights. The word *deckle* also describes the arrangement on the wet end of a paper machine which determines the width of the paper web.

density (1) In typesetting, the degree of blackness of type. The control of density is a matter of great concern to quality-oriented typographers. If there is too little density, the type can be "washed away" in shooting the film. If there is too much, letters can appear to fill in. And if the density does not match from day to day, it becomes impossible to strip in correction patches unless the corrections are set at the same time as the original copy. (2) In papermaking, density refers to the weight of paper compared to its volume; it is also related to a paper's absorbency, stiffness, and opacity. High density often indicates high strength. (3) In printing, it refers to the amount of ink coverage on the sheet.

die A design, letters, or pattern cut in metal for stamping, embossing, or die-cutting.

die-cutting The use of sharp steel rules to cut special shapes, such as labels, boxes, and containers, from printed or unprinted material. Die-cutting can be done on flatbed or rotary presses.

digital photography The use of a camera to make photographs recorded in pixels rather than a continuous tone image.

digital typesetter A typesetting machine that produces letters by drawing them out of computer memory, as opposed to photographing them through a lens. The principal advantages of digital typesetting are speed; better control of density; better base alignment; no possibility of having letters on a film master damaged or dirtied; the ability to have more typefaces and characters on-line; the ability to condense, expand, or slant any type electronically; and access to many more sizes of type.

digitizing The transferring of the original camera materials into a computer for off-line editing or graphics in a printed piece.

director Creative style and execution of a video or film are the responsibility of the director. He communicates his vision through his department heads to achieve the look and feel of the video.

dirty proof Any proof that contains many uncorrected errors, either marked or unmarked.

disk The medium used to store information from the computer.

display type In composition, display type is set larger than the text. It is meant to attract attention, such as headlines.

dissolve A dissolve is a cross fade, with the out-going scene going out and the in-coming scene coming in.

dolly A platform on wheels that a camera can be mounted on so that it can be rolled around.

dot etching Handwork on engravings and lithographic screened (halftone) negatives for correcting tonal values in either black-and-white or color work.

dot slurring Smearing of halftone dots.

dot spread Occurs when halftone dots print larger than they should, creating darker tones and colors.

dots, halftone The individual subdivisions of a printed surface created with a halftone screen.

draw-down   A term used to describe an ink chemist's method of roughly determining color shade. A small glob of ink is placed on paper and drawn down with the edge of a putty knife or spatula, to get a thin film of ink.

drilling   Punching of holes in folded sections, trimmed or untrimmed, or in finished books, which will permit their insertion over rings or posts in a binder.

drop-out   A halftone that contains no dots or detail in the highlights.

dryer   An oven through which the web passes after it leaves the last printing unit, used with heat-set inks. It heats the web at about 350 degrees Fahrenheit using gas, electricity, or steam to dry the ink vehicles. Air blasts are used to dry off volatile gases, resulting in higher temperature setting for ink. Also called *drying oven*.

drying time   The time it takes for an ink to become rub- or tack-free.

dub house   A company that makes duplicate videotapes from the duplication masters.

dubs   Duplicate copies of the duplication master video tape.

duplication master   A copy of the edit master used for final duplication of the videotape.

dubbing master   The original videotape from which duplications are made.

dummy   (1) A preliminary drawing or layout showing the position of illustrations and text as they are to appear in the final reproduction. (2) A set of blank pages made up in advance to show the size, shape, form and general style of a piece of printing.

duotone   A common printing technique by which a halftone is printed in two ink colors—most often black and another color.

duplex paper   A sheet of paper or cover stock with a different color on each side, usually produced by laminating.

duplicate transparency   The reproduction of a photograph in transparency form.

DVE (Digital Video Effects)   DVE is a special effects unit used to create many of the special visual effects on video tape.

edit masters   Master tapes with everything on them needed for the first duplication of a video, including audio, video, animation and graphics.

embossing   A process performed after printing in order to stamp a raised or depressed image (artwork or typography) into the surface of the paper, using engraved metal embossing dies, extreme pressure, and heat. Embossing styles include blind, deboss, and foil-embossed.

emulsion side   The side of a photographic film to which the emulsion is applied and on which the image is developed; the side on which scratching or scribing can be done. The emulsion side has a dull appearance.

enamel paper   A high-gloss, coated paper (either one side or two sides), also referred to simply as *coated paper.*

engraving   The raised image on the printing plate created by etching away the nonprinting area.

executive producer   The head of the production company who is totally responsible for the video or film project in all aspects is the executive producer. He is not involved in day-to-day arrangements or operations.

FOB (free on board)   Without charge for delivery to and placing on board a carrier at a specified point; the point from which shipping charges are calculated.

fast-drying ink   An ink that dries soon after printing.

felt finish   Surface characteristics of paper formed at the wet end of a paper machine, using woven wool and synthetic felts with distinctive patterns to create a similar texture in the finished sheets. Also called *felt mark, genuine felt finish,* or *felt marked finish.*

film   A thin, transparent plastic sheet that is coated with a photographic emulsion. After exposure, it is developed and processed to produce either a negative or a positive.

finished art   The final art that is to be placed before the camera (also called *mechanical, paste-up* or *production art*).

fireman   If special effects are being used that could potentially be a fire hazard, a fireman may be on-site as a precaution.

flags   Flags are solid black material on a frame designed to keep light from falling on a certain part of a scene.

flop   To reverse a negative or positive image bringing the underside out on top. A negative that must be flopped has emulsion on the wrong side.

flush   "Even with"; usually refers to typeset copy.

foil   A tissue-like material in sheet or roll form covered on one side with a metallic coloring used for stamping.

format   General term for size, style, and appearance of a printed piece or many layouts that have repeated the elements. Also refers to the size of the medium used for shooting a film or video.

four-color process   The four basic colors of ink (yellow, magenta, cyan, and black), which reproduce full-color photographs or art.

GCR (Grey Component Replacement)   A color separation technique that utilizes the black printer for the neutral grey or achromatic portion of any color, instead of chromatic colors (yellow, magenta, and cyan).

gaffer   The gaffer is the head of the lighting department in a video or film production. He designs the lighting style and directs its execution.

galley   (1) A shallow tray used to hold metal type in hot metal composition. (2) Typeset material before it has been arranged into final page form. A first-pass proof, also called a *galley proof.*

gatefold   A four-page insert, having foldouts on either side of the center spread.

generation   Each succeeding stage in reproduction from the original copy.

ghosting   The undesirable appearance of faint replicas of printed images caused chemically or mechanically.

gloss   A paper's shine or luster which reflects light.

gradient   The change of color from dark to light.

graphic artist   Any visual artist working in the commercial art field.

graphic arts   In common usage, all components of the printing industry.

graphic designer   A professional graphic artist who works with the elements of typography, illustration, photography, and printing to create commercial communications tools such as brochures, advertising, signage, posters, slide shows, and book jackets. A visual problem solver.

grips   The grip crew is a rigging crew, in charge of everything from moving dollies and cranes to the stands that shield the lights. They are, to some degree, the laborers of the film set. However, to a greater degree, they enhance the visual effects created through lighting controls.

grip truck   A truck that transports equipment used on location.

hair   The hair stylist takes care of the washing, coloring, trimming and styling of the talent's hair, especially for star talent.

hairline register   The joining or butting of two or more colors, with no color overlapping.

halftone   A picture with gradations of tone, formed by dots of varying sizes.

helicopter pilot   The helicopter pilot must be very skilled in piloting the helicopter for aerial photographs. The pilot may be asked to fly the helicopter sideways, backwards, etc. to get a particular shot.

Heidelberg press A two-color press with a maximum sheet size of 20½" × 29"

Helvetica The name of the most common sans serif typeface, used in a wide variety of text and display applications and available in some twenty different versions.

hickey An imperfection in lithographic press work due to a number of causes, such as dirt on the press, hardened specks of ink, or any dry hard particle that has worked into the ink or onto the plate or offset blanket.

HMI Daylight balanced lights used for filming that generate large amounts of light with relatively low power usage.

home economist (food stylist) The home economist prepares food to be shot on a video or film set. The typical home economist knows where to purchase the items required to prepare the food and the dyes or the substitutes used to make the food look even more scrumptious. They also know all of the tricks for assembling and preparing food so that it looks appetizing through a camera lens.

honey wagon A vehicle such as a large bus or motor home used on location shoots for wardrobe changes and as rest room facilities.

imprint To print other information on a previously printed piece by running it through a press again.

justified Lines of text copy that are set flush to both the left and the right margins. The text in most books is justified.

kerning In typesetting, certain letter combinations closer together than usual to provide visual even spacing. In the absence of kerning, the machine visualizes each letter as a rectangular and gives it that full amount of space.

key grip The key grip is in charge of the grip crew, the rigging, dolly, and grip equipment.

laminated Coated with a clear plastic, or two separate sheets of paper joined together as a single sheet to provide a special thickness, special surfaces, or varying colors from side to side.

laser   A very intense beam of light that is focused in a precise manner to make tiny dots. Also used for precision cutting and perforating. Laser printers reproduce at a lower resolution than linotronic or image-setting devices.

laser printer   A type of printing device using xerography and laser beams to recreate images (type and graphics).

layout   (1) The sequence of printed and blank pages of a book for press imposition. (2) A designer's conception on paper, boards or computer, of how the final job will appear.

leading   The space between the lines of type, from baseline to baseline. Originally referred to the metal used to separate the lines of type when type was set by hand.

letterpress   A relief printing method. Printing is done from cast metal type or plates on which the image or printing areas are raised above the nonprinting areas. Ink rollers touch only the top surface of the raised area; the nonprinting areas are lower and do not receive ink. The inked image is transferred directly to the paper.

line drawing   A drawing containing no grays or middle tones. In general, any drawing that can be reproduced without the use of halftone techniques.

location scout   The location scout finds locations suitable for photography for any particular job and makes arrangements with the owner of the location for its use.

logo   A mark or symbol created for an individual, company, or product that translates the impression of the body it is representing into a graphic image.

M   Abbreviation for the quantity of 1,000.

make-ready   In printing presses, all work done prior to running; adjusting the feeder, grippers, side guide, putting ink in the fountain, etc. Also, in letterpress, the building up of the press form, so that the heavy and light areas print with the correct impression.

make-up There can be anywhere from one to many make-up artists on a set. Their responsibilities range from simple jobs such as keeping the shine off of the talent's nose to those as complex as creating a completely different look on a face or body (such as aging, scars, extra-terrestrial and so on).

matt camera A black and white camera that copies camera-ready art for use in the on-lines session of assembling a videotape.

mechanical separations Copy which utilizes overlays to indicate the position and register of each color to be printed.

media buyer The media buyer schedules and purchases all media where clients place advertising. Media buyers work for advertising agencies, media buying services or directly for clients.

medical technician A medical technician and ambulance will be on the set if stunts are performed or unusual or risky conditions exist.

mezzotint A method of engraving a copper or steel printing plate by scraping and burnishing it to produce effects of light and shadow. Also, a patterned screen used in offset lithography to create the same effect.

modem An interface that forms a communication link, usually using telephone lines to connect one computer system to another.

mottled finish An uneven finish characterized by high and low spots or glossy and dull areas on the paper roll suitable for use only one time.

negative A film image that reverses all dark and light values of a photographic film or print.

off-line editing The initial assemblage of the footage by the editor of a film or video. The off-line editor uses the script to assemble the best takes in consecutive order to produce a rough-cut version for review and approval.

offset lithography (photolithography, offset) The most common form of lithographic printing in which the image area and the nonimage area exist on the same plane (plate), separated by chemical repulsion. To print, the ink is "offset" (transferred) from the plate onto a rubber blanket and then to the paper.

on-line editing   The final, color corrected, frame accurate, editing process done prior to final duplicating of the video tapes. The process involves transferring selected scenes, in order, onto an edited master tape.

one-up, two-up, etc.   Printing one (two, three, etc.) impressions of a job at the same time.

original   The artwork, mechanical, or other material furnished for printing reproduction; usually refers to photographs or drawings for halftone reproduction.

out of register   (1) Descriptive of pages on both sides of the sheet which do not back up accurately. (2) Two or more colors are not in the proper position when printed one over the other; register does not "match."

outline halftone (silhouette halftone)   A halftone image that is outlined by removing the dots that surround it.

overheads   Overheads can be solid black or white, silks or scrims. They are very large and are held over the people being photographed. Typical overheads are 12" × 12", 20" × 20" or 40" × 40".

overlays   (1) One name for a kind of art copy in which the artist prepares drawings in black ink or equivalent on sheets of transparent acetate, one for each color ink to be used in the printing. (2) A sheet of thin paper used in the packing on the impression cylinder to increase the squeeze of type and paper in letterpress printing.

overrun   Copies printed in excess of the specified quantity.

PMS (Pantone Matching System)   An ink color system widely used in the graphic arts. There are approximately 500 basic colors for both coated and uncoated paper. The color number and formula for each color are shown beneath the color swatch in the PMS ink book.

pans   Rotating the axis of a camera right to left or left to right to change the view of the camera are pans.

pasteup   The manual assembling of type elements and art on art boards, into final page form, ready for photography.

patch chromes   patch proofs from individual scans. Color proofs for client approval before being stripped into position.

per diem   A day rate given to a professional by a client to complete a day's assignment.

perfect binding (adhesive binding)   An inexpensive bookbinding technique in which the pages are glued rather than sewn to the cover and used primarily for paperbacks, small manuals, telephone books, and the like.

perfector press   A press that prints both sides of the paper at the same time.

photostat   Quick and readable photocopy prints produced without using the lengthy film process—a timesaver. Often shortened to *stat.*

pica   A unit of typographic measurement used to express page and type dimensions, such as the width of margins or columns. One pica = 12 points. Also, the standard type size on a typewriter of six characters to the inch.

pinholes   Very small holes in the emulsion of negatives caused by dust or dirt on the original artboards. These specks can be opaqued on the film to prevent exposure when plates are made. These pinholes can also appear as a result of improper or uneven ink coverage on printed surfaces.

PICT   A low-resolution screen image used for position only.

pixel   A dot made by an electronic digital device, such as a scanner or computer. It is the smallest point that can be controlled on a screen. The resolution of a computer screen is determined by the number of pixels, the higher the number of pixels, the better the resolution (72 dpi = 72 pixels per linear inch; 300 dpi = 300 pixels per linear inch).

point   The unit of measure used in typography for sizing fonts, the distance between lines, or the weight (thickness) of rules (72 points = 1 inch; 12 points = 1 pica). Also, a unit of measure for paper thickness equaling 1/1000 of an inch (10 point paper = 10/1000 inch).

point-of-purchase display (or point-of-sale display)   An exhibit on a counter or floor used to display a product for consumer purchase. The display usually carries an advertising message to encourage sales.

policeman   Many city ordinances require a policeman on the set, especially if city streets are being used. He is there for the protection of the crew and to direct traffic or on-lookers around the set.

position only   A facsimile of an original piece of art used to indicate to the printer the exact position on the final film that the final shot of the art should be stripped into.

positive   In photography, film containing an image in which the dark and light values are the same as the original. The reverse of negative. When one is using paper prints or films, this refers to the photographic image in which the tones are normal to the eye.

pre-light day   The pre-light day is where the lighting and grip crew hang the lights and prepare for the filming days.

preseparated art   Art that has a separate overlay prepared for each color in the illustration.

press check   The client or a representative is usually present at the printing plant to give final approval of the press proofs.

press proof   Actual press sheets that show image, tone value, and color. A few sheets are run and a final check is made prior to printing the job.

press sheet   The full-size sheet of paper selected for a job to be printed on a sheet-fed press. The sheet size is usually slightly larger than the negative flat, to allow for gripper and trim margins.

process colors In printing, the subtractive primaries: yellow, magenta, and cyan, plus black in four-color process printing.

producer The producer makes all of the arrangements for the video production. He schedules crews, determines the length of the days and all of the requirements of the job. He controls and heads all of the operations in a managerial capacity.

production artist A professional artist who works with a designer in taking a layout through to mechanicals and often on through the printing process.

production assistant The production assistant is the "gofer" on the job assisting the video production staff in any way possible.

production coordinator The person responsible for making sure that everything is in order before it goes under the camera.

production manager The production manager works in an advertising agency or design studio. Their responsibilities include working with the artists to ensure that artwork is prepared properly for the printers and overseeing all printing of that artwork.

progressive color proofs (progs) Proofs of color separation negatives that have been exposed to offset plates and printed using process inks. They are assembled in the sequence of printing: (1) yellow plate alone, (2) red alone, (3) yellow and red, (4) blue alone, (5) yellow, red, and blue, (6) black alone; and (7) yellow, red, blue, and black. Progressive proofs are the preferred way for checking the color of the separation negatives using the same inks, paper, ink densities, and color sequence as intended for the production run.

prop master The prop master obtains or creates the props required for the video or film set at a studio or location setting.

protection master A copy of the edit master that is stored separately as a back-up of the completed videotape.

reels A reel of film (more commonly a video tape) that contains samples of one's personal work or that of the production company.

reflection copy (reflective art)   Original copy for reproduction that is on an opaque material and must be photographed by light reflected from its surface. Examples are photographs, paintings and dye-transfer prints.

register marks   Crosses or other marks applied to original copy prior to photography used for achieving perfect alignment (register) of negatives and color separations.

resolution   The number of dots per inch of a scanned image. Low-resolution scans are usually saved at less than 1 megabyte dpi (dots per inch) and are used for position only. High-resolution scans are usually saved at 200 dpi or higher and can be used for manipulation or editing.

reverse type (dropout type)   A printing style in which the background is the printed image and the characters remain the color of the paper.

rough-cut   The product achieved as a result of the off-line edits in the initial stage of video production.

runaround   In composition, the term describing a type area set in measures that are adjusted to fit around a picture or other element of the design.

sans serif   A style of typeface distinguished by the absence of serifs, or ticks, on the ends of strokes.

scanning   The process of (1) using a laser scanner to convert a continuous tone image into a halftone dot. Scanning is used to produce a halftone, duotone, tritone, quadtone, conventional four-color process separation, screen or vignette or (2) the process of digitizing an image to be saved on a computer file.

score   To impress a mark in a sheet of paper, usually cover stock, to make folding easier. Scoring is often necessary when a fold must be made against the paper's grain. Scoring with a dull rule is also called *creasing.*

screen   A sheet of glass or film having lines or other patterns. The conventional gravure screen has crossed lines; the contact screen has vignetted dots.

scrims   Scrims are a light screen designed to control the quality of light falling on a scene.

script   The script is the blueprint for the video or film project including all of the visual requirements and a complete narrative and audio description.

script clerk   The script clerk watches the script to make sure the talent is delivering the lines correctly. He or she takes notes of each scene and checks for continuity in appearances. For example, if a blue sweater is worn by the star in scene one, then he should be wearing the same sweater if scene 3 is the same day and location. Script notes are critical during the editing process.

set-off (offset)   The undesirable transfer of wet ink from one sheet to another.

sheet-fed press   A printing press that takes paper previously cut into sheets, as opposed to paper on a continuous roll.

sheet wise   In normal printing practice, the pages for one side of the sheet are locked on the press and the desired number of copies is printed. The plates are then removed and the plates for the other side of the sheet are locked on the press and the reverse side of the sheet is run the same number of impressions. This means to print 1000 copies of a backed-up sheet a press must make 2000 impressions.

signature   A single press sheet with 4, 8, 12, 16 or 32 pages printed on it so that when it folds it makes up a single unit, or book or, for example, part of a catalog. Several signatures can be stitched together to make one piece or trimmed and prepared for perfect binding.

silks   Silks are diffusion screens used to modify the quality of light coming from a lighting fixture and falling on an object.

slip-sheeting   The placement of pieces of paper between folded sections prior to trimming four sides, to separate completed books or units.

special effects   The special effects include anything used to enhance an image or provide a setting, from lightning bolts to smoke or fog.

spot varnish   Press varnish applied to a portion of the sheet, as opposed to an overall application of the varnish.

spread   (1) The photographic thickening of type characters or other printing details that will provide a color or tint overlap and allow for slight misregister in the successive printings. (2) Two facing pages in a brochure, booklet, or book.

stage manager   A person that is responsible for the total operation of the stage or facility.

storyboards   Quick sketches depicting highlights in the scenes of a script. They are used to present the ideas behind the script to the client.

stripper   The stripper assembles negatives in flats in preparation of making printing plates.

sweetening   The mixing of narration, music, special effects and original dialogue onto a tape so that it can be laid back to the original master.

tabloid   The page size of a newspaper, approximately 11¾" wide and from 15" to 17" long (approximately one-half of a standard-size newspaper page).

teacher/welfare worker   On all sets using talent under the age of 18 a teacher/welfare worker must be in attendance. There must be one teacher for every 10 persons under the age of 18 for any given day of work. This requirement is part of the child labor laws and contains very strict penalties if it is not adhered to.

TelePrompTer   The TelePrompTer is a computer screen on the front of a camera lens for the talent to read. It contains the on-camera script lines for the talent and is typically used on soap-operas or news programs.

TIFF (Tagged image file format) A format for saving scanned images. Once saved, these images can be edited on the computer.

tissue overlay (1) A sheet of tissue covering a piece of artwork or the like on which the designer may refer to particular areas of the copy with instructions to the engraver or printer. (2) A protective tissue covering for camera copy.

traffic manager Mid-size and larger advertising agencies employ a traffic manager to ensure that all schedules are met in the production of projects.

trap The printing of one ink over another. Also, the creation of hairline overlaps to ensure proper registration in printing.

treatment A short synopsis of the creative approach to a film or video is known as the treatment.

typeface A style or design of type encompassing shape, weight and proportions which make it distinct from other typefaces. Also called a *font.*

typeface family A group of typefaces that are similar in style, usually differing only in boldness and whether characters are straight (Roman) or inclined slightly (Italic).

varnish A thin, protective coating applied to a printed sheet for protection or appearance. Also, in inkmaking, it can be all or part of the ink vehicle.

video assist The images captured by a video camera, synchronized with those of a film camera and shown on a film monitor at one time.

video assist operator When shooting film, a video camera is attached to the film camera so that clients visiting the set can view, through the lens of the film camera, and get an idea what the project will look like. The video assist operator operates this camera and playback unit.

vignette The softening of edges on an image from dark to light, usually ending at a zero percent dot. Also, an ornamental border.

voice over   The audio narration in a video or film in which the speaker is not seen on camera.

VTR   The abbreviation for video tape recorder.

wardrobe   The person in charge of the wardrobe selects all of the clothing and accessories. It is their responsibility that all items are taken care of, whether it be storage, cleaning or mending.

washup   The process of cleaning the rollers, form, or plate, and sometimes the ink fountain of a press.

web printing (roll-fed printing)   A generic term for any printing method in which paper is fed into the press from continuous rolls as opposed to flat sheets.

widow   The last line of a paragraph which does not extend to the right margin and appears as the first line on a page. Generally an indication of poor page makeup and is often avoided by running pages a line long or a line short or revising the text. Also a single word, or a part of a word in a line by itself.

work-and-turn, work-and-twist, work-and-tumble   Work-and-turn (or *work-and-twist*) is a technique whereby the plates for both sides of the sheet are locked side by side and run for half the desired number on a double-size sheet. The plates are left in the same position, the printed sheets are turned over right or left (or in *work-and-tumble,* end for end) run through the press again, this time printing the reverse side. This method permits 1,000 copies to be printed on both sides using only 1,000 impressions.

work-and-flop (W & F)   A printing layout for printing both the front and back of a sheet from a single plate. After the first run through the press, the printed pile of sheets is inverted, so the tail edge becomes the gripper edge for printing the back side of the sheets; also called *work-and-tumble.*

wrap   The completion of a video filming day is a wrap. It signifies the beginning of the break-down process, including the break-down of the cameras and returning the components to their proper cases, break-down of the lighting and its placement in the truck or proper storage place, break-down of the set and returning the stage to its original condition.

zoom   To zoom is to change the optical point of a lens from a wide shot to a telephoto or vice versa.

INDEX

TITLES OF INTEREST IN
PRINT AND BROADCAST MEDIA

For further information or a current catalog, write:
NTC Business Books
a division of *NTC Publishing Group*
4255 West Touhy Avenue
Lincolnwood, Illinois 60646–1975